Literacy

A Handbook for
Development Workers

Paul Fordham
Deryn Holland
Juliet Millican

Oxfam
(UK and Ireland)
Voluntary Service Overseas

First published by Oxfam UK and Ireland 1995

Reprinted by Oxfam GB 1998, 2000

© Voluntary Service Overseas 1995

ISBN 0 85598 315 9

A catalogue record for this publication is available from the British Library.

Available from the following agents:
for the USA: Stylus Publishing LLC, PO Box 605, Herndon, VA 20172-0605
tel 800 232 0223; fax 703 661 1501; email styluspub@aol.com
for Canada: Fernwood Books Ltd., PO Box 9409, Stn. A, Halifax,
Nova Scotia B3K 5S3
tel 902 422 3302; fax 902 422 3179; email fernwood@istar.ca
for southern Africa: David Philip Publishers, PO Box 23408, Claremont,
Cape Town 7735, South Africa
tel +27 (0)21 64 4136; fax +27 (0)21 64 3358; email dpp@iafrica.com
for Australia: Bushbooks, PO Box 1958, Gosford, NSW 2250
tel 02 4323 3274; fax 02 9212 2468; email bushbook@ozemail.com.au

For the rest of the world, contact
Oxfam Publishing, 274 Banbury Road, Oxford OX2 7DZ, UK.
tel + 44 (0)1865 311311; fax + 44 (0)1865 313925; email publish@oxfam.org.uk

Published by Oxfam GB
274 Banbury Road, Oxford OX2 7DZ, UK
(registered as a charity, no. 202918)

in association with Voluntary Service Overseas
317 Putney Bridge Road, London SW15 2PN, UK
(registered as a charity, no. 313757)

All photographs supplied by Oxfam Photo Library
Printed by Oxfam Print Unit

Oxfam GB is a member of Oxfam International.

Contents

A note from the publishers

The need for an adult literacy handbook was identified by VSO (Voluntary Service Overseas), whose volunteers have been working in countries throughout the developing world since the late 1950s. The idea has been developed in collaboration with Oxfam (UK and Ireland), and the resulting text draws on the experience of both organisations, and the work they support in Bangladesh, China, Ghana, Honduras, India, Mali, Nepal, Nicaragua, South Africa, and Tanzania, and the experience of others working in the field, throughout the developing world.

About the authors

Paul Fordham was Director of Adult Education at the University of Southampton for 18 years, and is now Honorary Professor in the International Centre for Education in Development at the University of Warwick. His publications include *Learning Networks: Non-Formal Education on a Housing Estate* (with Poulton and Randle), (Routledge and Kegan Paul); *Participation, Learning, and Change* (Commonwealth Secretariat); and *Co-operating for Literacy* (ICAE/DSE).

Deryn Holland is Assistant Education Officer (Staff Development), Buckinghamshire County Council. She works locally and internationally as a trainer, researcher, and writer in adult education and literacy. Her publications include *The Progress Profile* (Adult Literacy Basic Skills Unit) and *Developing Literacy and Numeracy: An Intermediate Pack for Trainers* (The Open University).

Juliet Millican has worked in Adult Education for most of her own adult life, and in literacy for the past ten years, both overseas and in the UK. She is currently co-ordinator of Access Courses at Hastings College. Her publications include *Reading, Writing, and Cultivating: A Handbook for Post-Literacy Workers* (CESO), a guidebook for the management of a credit fund, and a variety of teaching materials.

Acknowledgements

Many colleagues, too numerous to mention, have helped to shape the ideas on which this book is based. They will recognise their own contributions; if we have not acknowledged them individually, it is because their insights have passed into common currency among workers in the field of adult literacy. We must, however, acknowledge our particular debt to Alan Rogers and Brian Street for their contributions to literacy work, and our debt to all those involved in a recent research project commissioned by the Overseas Development Administration ('Using Literacy: A New Approach to Post-Literacy Materials').

Especial thanks are due also to Sandy Fury of the University of Warwick, for creating order out of the chaos of our barely compatible computer discs; to Rachel Yates, for allowing us to draw on her bibliography; and to the Adult Literacy Basic Skills Unit (ALBSU) for permission to reproduce material from *The Progress Profile*.

We are also grateful to the VSO volunteers and Oxfam workers, and overseas staff of both organisations, who shared with us their first-hand experiences of planning and implementing literacy programmes. Above all, we thank the learners in many countries who have taught us most of what we know about what it means to be literate, and how to go about acquiring the skills which (like most people who have been formally educated) we tend to take for granted.

Paul Fordham, Deryn Holland, and Juliet Millican

Foreword

I feel honoured to be invited to write a Foreword to this book, which I have read with great interest. I particularly welcome three of its key messages. The first is that we should not exaggerate either the disadvantages experienced by those who cannot read or write, or the advantages which learning to read or write brings. There are, of course, significant benefits to be gained from learning literacy skills. But, as the authors of this book point out, many non-literate persons can lead fulfilled lives; and many who learn to read and write may still find that they are cheated — and in particular that they are still poor! As literacy workers, we will achieve much more if our expectations are realistic.

The second key message of this book is its insistence that literacy is something we *do*, not just something we *learn*. The authors aim to help men and women to read and to write in their everyday lives. They are mostly and inevitably concerned with what happens in the classroom; but they never forget that what takes place there is of no value, unless it leads to real reading and real writing outside the classroom. This means that all teaching for literacy will need to start with real life (using real literacy situations, practices, and events in the community) and end with real life. Unless our teaching is based on reality, we shall have produced learners like the woman from Nepal (quoted in Chapter 4), who said that she could read the literacy primer, but nothing else. And that is no use to her at all. All this means, as this book indicates, that training for literacy is not just a matter of developing skills. It is more a question of developing the right attitudes, especially building up learners' confidence. This is often overlooked in literacy training programmes today.

Thirdly, I value this book's emphasis on the fact that literacies vary from group to group. It is not just that they vary from country to country and culture to culture. Fishing communities have different literacy practices from trading communities, for example; indeed, one group of fisherpeople can have quite different concerns from another group along the same coast. Urban and rural literacy contexts are quite different and call for different approaches. This must mean that teaching literacy skills is always a matter of innovation: making up things as we go along.

For this reason, readers are invited to use this handbook creatively, rather than let it constrain them. It is planned as a 'useful problem-solving resource', leading readers to decide for themselves what to do in any situation. It asks readers not to follow it, but to *use* it.

I feel sure that planners and trainers with or without professional qualifications in the teaching of literacy will find this book helpful. Oxfam and VSO are to be congratulated on identifying a long-felt need and working so hard with the authors to fulfil it.

Alan Rogers
Education for Development
Reading
England

Preface

The purpose of this book

This is a book for development workers with no formal training in adult education or literacy who encounter the need for literacy in the communities with which they work. It looks at the relationship between literacy and development, the role of literacy in development, and the importance of literacy to development. By exploring some of the central issues and debates, we aim to help development workers to listen with more understanding to requests for literacy from the people with whom they are working. For example:

An agricultural extension worker may find farmers who are beginning to experiment with new methods. They will need to record information on their yields or on varying prices at the market. ...

... A health worker may be faced with requests from mothers at a clinic who want to understand the child-growth charts or the words on immunisation certificates. ...

... A co-operative development worker may start by introducing book-keeping to someone who is already literate, but may find other members of the co-operative wanting to read the information recorded. ...

... A community development worker may want to help village-group members who are promoting a local project, like sinking a new well, to develop their leadership skills.

To respond effectively to such situations, we need not only some knowledge of teaching and learning methods, but also an understanding of some of the consequences of introducing literacy to individuals, groups, or communities.

When people request 'literacy', they will have their own idea of what they want, and their own way of assimilating it into their lives. This book aims to help both learners and development workers to understand what literacy means to them, why they have asked for it, what kind of literacy they want, and what purposes they expect it to serve. Helping learners to understand these questions is the best way for development workers to deepen their own understanding of different literacies and literacy practices; and to move on from seeing reading and writing merely as skills to be learned in a mechanical way.

It is important to recognise that there is no one literacy which people either have or do not have. For one person, reading or counting may be more important than writing. For another, writing a simple letter to an absent relative may be a sufficient achievement. Traders will want yet another kind of literacy. The question of what language to choose for literacy in multi-lingual situations is perhaps one of the most difficult to answer, and will mean considering the relationship between language and power.

Most of this book is essentially practical. It looks at the various stages in planning, teaching, and evaluating a small-scale literacy programme, and the likely effects, both on individuals and on the progress of development in an area. It offers suggestions for using available materials and for developing new ones designed for specific situations or places. It is not intended to be a comprehensive guide; nor does it set out to be a complete course book for the training of trainers. It is designed to set the reader thinking about what to do, and to give examples of how things have happened in other places. We hope that the ideas and examples it contains will be an essential foundation for readers who are trying to decide how to meet what for them may be an unfamiliar request. It should also help development workers to decide for themselves when it might be appropriate to suggest a literacy component in a local development project.

'Deciding for oneself' is a major theme of this book. Real problems can only be solved and real choices can only be made by the people who are experiencing them. Ideas from elsewhere can be a useful stimulus; but they cannot provide ready-made answers or recipes for instant success. However, by considering some of the recurring issues in the learning and teaching of literacy, and looking at some of the implications behind policy decisions, we hope that readers will understand their own particular situations better. Seeing how other people have introduced literacy into development programmes might inspire confidence in another community's ability to do the same.

We have written a resource book, not an academic textbook. It is to be used in practical situations, either by development workers who decide to begin some literacy teaching themselves, or by those who plan larger programmes and employ local teachers. We hope it will be relevant to decision-makers, planners, trainers, and teachers.

It would be wrong for a short and practical book like this to gloss over the complexities of literacy. At the same time, there is no mystery about it. On each and every occasion, there are four crucial questions for development workers to consider.

- Who needs literacy?
- What do they need it for?
- What kind of literacy do they need?
- How will the programme be planned and implemented?

We hope that this book will help development workers to understand the implications behind each of these choices.

PART ONE

Literacy and Development

Tanzania: Preparing to open a bank account for a cattle-dip project, a woman from Naisinyai village practises signing her name, watched by a worker from the Maasai Health Services Project.
Photo: Geoff Sayer

CHAPTER 1

The case for literacy

People often assume that there are absolute states of being literate or illiterate. This idea leads to the belief that a person who is illiterate can be led through a series of simple steps (with a few tests along the way), leading from one absolute state to another. After that, the previous lack of knowledge and skills which prevented him or her from being productively involved in development will have disappeared, and as a newly literate person he or she will become a fully functioning and knowledgeable member of the community.

This notion was always a myth, but it persists, and can be seen in statements or slogans which talk about the 'eradication' of illiteracy, as though it were a disease like smallpox. The myth is promoted by those who have been formally educated (like all the readers and writers of this book), who tend to deny the wisdom and competence of the unschooled. Many people assume that, once the skills of reading and writing are acquired, lives will be transformed.

We probably all know cases of successful non-literate people. For example, Paul Fordham's paternal great-grandmother was a competent dressmaker, raised four children, all of whom went to school, and died in 1917 at the age of 89. She was certainly illiterate at the time of her marriage in 1856, and it seems likely that she remained so. She grew up just before the start of mass literacy in Britain.

In the modern world, there seems little doubt that it is always better to be able to read and to write than not to have these skills. Acquiring them can and should transform people's lives; but the timing has to be right, and the process must take account of the learners' social context. These issues are examined in later parts of this chapter and in Part Two.

One of the advantages of learning to be literate is the increase in confidence which it brings, both to individuals and to their communities. In the aftermath of the Tanzanian literacy campaign of the 1970s, Yusuf Kassam analysed eight conversations with newly literate people.[1] They all emphasised the sense of self-confidence which they had gained. One person recorded: *'Now that I have become literate, I feel that before I was carrying a small lantern, but now a pressure lamp has been brought to me ... I don't feel inferior.'*

In the same analysis, one learner recorded how, as a non-literate person, he had been *'made to work like a plough'*. He described the sense of personal liberation brought by literacy: it was as though *'the rope that had been twisted around me was untied, and so naturally I felt happy'*. He went on to say: *'We can defend our rights; we can't be forced to do anything against our own wishes; we can't be cheated.'* Increased confidence often has social and political significance, besides the personal benefits which it brings.

Testimonies collected more recently in Bolivia echo those from Tanzania. Women learners in a shanty town outside La Paz explained that they went to classes *'So we won't be cheated'* ... *'So that we won't have to say that we don't know how to sign our names'* ... *'So we can help our children with their homework'* ... *'So we'll know who to vote for'.*[2]

Motivation for literacy

Evaluations of literacy programmes often report that learners lack motivation or that the number of drop-outs is large. A reporter from the current Indian national programme (National Literacy Mission) recorded in one of the 'low-performing districts' (Himachel Pradesh) that, while about 26 per cent of the community had enrolled, more than one third had dropped out before the end of the course. Official attitudes were supportive; slogans on bus windscreens declared: *Now there will be no more illiterates.* But the intended learners did not read the slogans, and, in spite of the high degree of motivation among the professional staff, 'There is a general dearth of volunteer teachers at the grassroots level, and village-level committees are practically defunct.' The writer calls for 're-planning, based on thorough soul-searching'.[3]

Such disappointment is common, and not just in India. The history of many of the world's large-scale literacy schemes has been one of failure. The 1967-72 Experimental World Literacy Programme (EWLP), sponsored by UNESCO, is just one example.[4] Only in Tanzania, with strong and persistent political leadership, was the EWLP a success. A dynamic movement for political change lies behind other large-scale success stories, in most cases after revolutionary change (as in the Soviet Union, Cuba, and Nicaragua).

The preface to this book stated that the planning and implementation of literacy projects requires firm decisions on four key questions:

- Who needs literacy?
- What do they need it for?
- What kind of literacy do they need?
- How will the programme be planned and implemented?

In all the successful large-scale cases there was clear agreement:

- Literacy was for everybody.
- The purposes were both political (consolidating revolutionary gains) and economic (providing an educated work-force for the new command economies).
- All was to be done via the national language and a clearly structured, hierarchical organisation.

*Nicaragua:
After the revolution
in 1979, 95,000
students, factory
workers, and civil
servants volunteered
to run literacy classes
in poor communities.
It is claimed that in
six months over
400,000 adults
learned to read and
write.*
Photo: Mike Goldwater

In the later 1990s, development workers are more likely to be concerned with local initiatives and less with the transformation of whole societies than they were twenty or thirty years ago. Literacy *can* be a transforming experience, both for individuals and for societies. But the timing of its introduction has to be carefully considered, and any programme has to be firmly embedded in its time and place. In the words of Om Shrivastava, working in adult education in India, when is the 'magic moment' for literacy? When and how can good motivation be assumed or generated?[5]

When to introduce literacy

To understand the right timing for a literacy programme, we need to understand how and where literacy will support other aspects of development. This is the most important question for field workers when deciding on timing. Whether or not the 'magic moment' has arrived may well depend on how literacy skills are likely to affect other aspects of development.

In Honduras a co-operative union was formed, with the aim of challenging unjust forms of land ownership. However, it was difficult for members without literacy to take part in union business, and to understand legal and contractual rights regarding land. When the union decided to deal with the problem of land ownership, a recognition of the need for literacy followed close behind: the first was not possible without the second.

In Bangladesh, with the help of Oxfam, villagers set up a Community Development Association in order to implement a loan scheme. Villagers all paid into the loan scheme on a regular basis and then were able to borrow larger amounts from it, to pay for the inputs they needed to grow sugar and wheat. The profit they made from selling their harvest enabled them to repay loans into the revolving fund; but in order to manage the credit facilities, all members had to understand basic book-keeping. The need for credit led to the need for villagers to attend a literacy programme.

There are few societies where literacy does not bring more power (both personal and social), more ability to take part fully in society, and more opportunities for personal and social growth and development of all kinds. Nevertheless, the failures of many attempts to introduce literacy underline the need to ensure that the timing is right, and the importance of answering our four key questions.

Development can and does sometimes happen without literacy. For example, radio broadcasts, or group discussions, or demonstrations by an extension agent may be enough for some kinds of agricultural extension. But experience shows that, sooner or later, as the economy becomes more complex and basic services improve, development agencies and potential learners will see a need for literacy skills. And this argument — a strictly economic one — is quite separate from the more idealistic arguments in support of promoting literacy, like enabling people to read the Koran or the Bible, or believing that literacy is a basic human right. But the idealistic arguments sometimes have to be supported by economic ones, especially when trying to persuade funding agencies that a literacy programme is worthwhile or good value for money.

Why is literacy important? Would it not be better to concentrate on increasing employment and production? The answer to this question is that, while it is useless to offer literacy *instead of* food, housing, clean water, electricity, or jobs, it may become uneconomic to offer them *without* it. Literacy may be only a part, but it is still an essential part, of the range of basic services which bring direct economic returns as well as direct social benefits.

A VSO volunteer in Nigeria found that the community in which she worked as a nurse began to organise its own literacy programme, after she had formed a village health committee. The committee members took their tasks seriously, and decided that they needed literacy to carry out their role properly. A primary school, recently constructed for the children, provided the venue, and the learners paid for a teacher between themselves.

Lack of pure water and/or miles of walking to fetch it leaves less time for production and increases the likelihood of illness. Lack of vaccination, health education and basic curative services leaves workers ... too weak to be fully productive ... Illiteracy reduces workers' flexibility and productivity even in 'simple' occupations such as peasant farming, construction or handicrafts.[6]

It is pointless to offer literacy courses instead of the more expensive roads, water, and other basic services, because 'without the motivation of the learner, nothing is going to happen. The effects of the campaign will disappear as rapidly as the posters announcing its launching will fade.'[7] But deciding when to introduce literacy classes is the essential first step in helping to ensure that learners are motivated to learn.

Participation

The fact that people can and do plan and instigate their own development programmes is often overlooked by professional agencies. Recently the idea of 'participation', or the planned involvement of community members in decision-making, has been presented as a new approach. But the idea is not new in the field of adult education. In early twentieth-century England, students in classes promoted by the Workers' Educational Association successfully demanded a voice in the design of curricula and the appointment of teaching staff. In many universities in the Western world in the 1960s, student movements promoted 'participation' as one of the key ideas behind their demands for change in the way universities were administered.

This book takes the view that learners themselves, as well as agencies and field workers, will and should have their own view of what should be done: they should be full participants at all levels of decision making. Their views may be different from the view of an outsider, however well informed he or she may be. If the views of insiders are not taken into account, it is unlikely that the outsider will design a programme that can achieve lasting results.

Programmes that involve users in their design, conception, and organisation are intended to encourage people to reflect more deeply on their own lives, and to take more control over them. However, some words of caution are necessary. Participation has become a widely popular concept, but we have to ask what it means. A recent study commissioned by UNCHS points out that community participation can mean at least three different things.[8] It can mean:

- *contributing* (where money, labour, or materials are provided);
- *consulting* (where views are sought in order to elicit contributions, but the decisions may be made elsewhere);
- or *controlling* (where community members are really performing community-management functions).

Development agencies often claim to practise the third kind of participation, when in reality they concede only the first or the second. Field workers should consider very carefully the sense in which they actually use this concept.

The kind of participation which we advocate in this book is intended to promote changes in people's lives in ways they can believe in. Many programmes have similar aims, but in fact it may be the underlying goals and assumptions of the planners (the outsiders), rather than those of the users (the insiders), that determine the direction of those changes.

In this book, we envisage a certain kind of participatory programme:

- one which recognises, values, and uses the contribution of everyone in the community;
- which recognises people's individual differences, rather than assuming that they are all the same;
- which offers information, rather than seeking to persuade people to make certain choices;
- which accepts that the knowledge of insiders is worth as much as that of outsiders;
- which seeks to exchange that information on an equal basis, where learners will also be teachers and teachers will also be learners;
- which takes a holistic approach, keeping in mind the physical, emotional, and learning needs of a community;
- which does not start from the belief that a literate society is in any way 'superior' to an oral society;
- and, finally, one which does not seek to work towards goals imported from outside by the planners, but is free to follow the learning needs of the community which it intends to serve.[9]

What kind of literacy?

Up to this point, we have avoided any attempt to define what we mean by literacy. The reason is that there is no one literacy acceptable for all time, for all people, and for all places. Most writers on the subject now tend to talk of *literacies*, rather than one state of being literate. Consider two examples, from very different societies.

In St Vincent in 1975, it was decided to prepare a plan for 'adult education'. The initial brief, although wide, had no particular emphasis on literacy, because schooling was thought to be widely available. An international consultant was hired to write the first proposals and began to look at the issue of unemployment. He called a meeting of the Bel Air Small Farmers' Union to discuss marketing problems. After some time, he noticed that there were more people outside the room listening in than there were inside and participating. He was told that these were the illiterate members who were 'too ashamed' to come in. They had been to school in the past, but had either never learned to be literate or had forgotten what they had learned. The result was a proposal for functional

In a recent evaluation of literacy classes in Uganda, it was discovered that the range of needs expressed might lead to the provision of different kinds of literacy. Immigrants into Buganda might want to improve their spoken and written competence in the local *lingua franca* (Luganda), in which the classes were conducted. Native Luganda speakers might need a different approach to a language they could already speak, but in which they could neither read nor write. Others aspired to speak and be literate in the language of commerce and government (in this case mostly English). The government itself considered that a first priority should be to encourage use of the language used by the security forces (Swahili).

literacy, based on new crops and approaches. This involved simply written handbooks on keeping rabbits and marketing crops. Farmers needed to increase their personal confidence by becoming literate, and in order to participate in the business of the collective of small farmers.[10]

In 1986 in the UK, the same consultant thought it was time to learn how to use a word processor and decided that the first step should be to buy one and practise a little self-instruction. He sought advice from the computer supplier, and began to explore a range of hardware and software options. After a mutually frustrating dialogue, the assistant exclaimed, 'We do expect our customers to be computer-literate — Sir.' The development consultant began to understand a little better the humiliation felt by people who are labelled as 'illiterate'; he knew a lot about books, but nothing about computers, and the scornful shop assistant was a deterrent to further self-instruction. In most societies, standards of what is meant by literacy are in rapid change. It has become easy for anyone to experience at first hand that there is no one literacy.

The question *'What kind of literacy?'* cannot be answered until the context is thoroughly understood and there is an answer to the first two of the four key questions for planners: *Who needs it?* and *What do they need it for?*

One way of defining literacy might be to say that for any one person it requires *an ability to communicate through reading and writing all that can be understood and communicated through speech.* But this leaves too many questions unanswered for it to be universally accepted and would not, for example, cover the person who wants to learn another language at the same time as becoming literate. UNESCO defines a literate person as *one who can with understanding both read and write a short simple statement on his everyday life.*

What is functional?

Literacy specialists often insist that literacy must be 'functional'. What does this mean? It is easy to give examples of what is not functional. For instance, a water-catchment project which used voluntary female labour plus paid male masons held a literacy class under a tree. The women learned to write a few words related to the project (such as *water, well, dam*) in their own mother-tongue. But, because the classes were not taken seriously enough to be held regularly, there was no evidence of learning to read sentences, even after a year of classes. And the women were in no better position to contribute to the catchment programme just by learning to read and write a few words. Moreover, their particular mother-tongue is not often seen in written form. The written words they would see in their daily lives, such as advertisements, or government notices, were likely to be in the local *lingua franca* (in this case Swahili), or in English (the language of the elite, of formal business enterprise, and the major newspapers). So what seemed a clear and simple decision to promote 'functional' literacy turned out to have complex implications which had not been considered in advance. The literacy component of this water programme seemed unlikely to be very useful, either in improving the practical project or in advancing the learners' reading and writing skills; unless, of course, there were fundamental changes in perceptions and organisation. So what steps can be taken, both to make literacy functional and to make some contribution to other aspects of development?

The question of whether or not literacy is functional depends on the context; that is, it has to be re-defined for every time and in every place. In the example given in the previous paragraph, it could be argued that literacy would help development, if the women were learning to be part of project management, as well as providing cheap labour; and if the language used was one in which they could read information useful to the project. (This is the highly political question of language choice.) Sharing the management of the project would have to be built in at the project-planning stage, as part of a policy to increase community self-management capabilities (sometimes called 'capacity building'). A different choice of language might also increase individual motivation to learn (because it would be more useful) and therefore increase the general level of understanding and willingness to change ways of life. Both would make a significant difference to the lives of the women, and the income they could earn. In any context, there is a complex interaction both between different aspects of development (such as water, health, agricultural development, education) and between development and literacy: the latter is never a simple technology and cannot be planned as if it were.

However, there are some general guidelines — often based on past mistakes — which can help development workers to think about what to do. These general guidelines are considered below. Above all, the starting point has to be *asking questions about purposes*.

Changing ideas about what is functional

In the past, what was thought to be 'functional' was seen in a rather simplistic way. In the 1960s, for example, UNESCO promoted the Experimental World Literacy Programme, which tried to add a literacy component to particular economic development projects. It failed to ask certain crucial questions.

- What is the purpose of literacy in this project?
- When should it be introduced?
- How should it be planned and taught?
- What language should be used?

In the 1960s it sometimes seemed enough to say that farmers in an agricultural development project would need to read the instructions on the fertiliser bags; but this ignored what the farmers themselves wanted, and was one of the reasons for widespread failures in the EWLP. Contemporary ideas of development assumed that more and better education (as determined by educational and development planners) would lead directly to economic growth and so, less directly, to increased human welfare. For some lucky individuals, in the right place at the right time, it worked; for the majority, it did not.

In the 1970s, literacy in development sometimes became more overtly political and aimed at the total transformation ('liberation') of whole societies. The writings of the Brazilian educator and philosopher, Paulo Freire, were used to widen the idea of what was functional, to include political, social, and cultural purposes as well as economic ones. The relative success of mass literacy campaigns in post-revolutionary societies (such as Nicaragua) led some enthusiasts to recommend such campaigns as appropriate for all developing countries. But this enthusiasm tended to obscure the fact that, as we have already noted, the purposes of the successful mass campaigns were, first, to help ensure the rapid growth of new command economies, planned and operated by the new political States; and, second, to ensure a new and centralised political unity after revolutionary change. The purposes of the later 1990s, and therefore our ideas of functionality and appropriate methods, are likely to be different. We are now more concerned with local literacies and languages than with centralised national agendas. And we talk less of 'liberation' in the global sense, although the word is still used in some circumstances, especially where women are concerned.

'Every house a classroom. Every table a desk. Every Nicaraguan a teacher!' A poster promoting the national literacy crusade, 1981.

11

So international ideas about what is functional have changed with what is seen as appropriate for 'development'. As long ago as 1974, the World Bank noted that the 'human capital' approach to development had been changed, and that the term now embraced questions of employment (or lack of it), environment, social equality, and participation. A UNESCO monograph in 1992 goes further and argues that making literacy functional implies placing people at the centre of their environment and giving them the means to take an active part in community life.[11] It is also argued that development must be 'sustainable', which means two things: that local communities must acquire the capacity to carry on and develop themselves when outside agencies have left, and that development should not have a negative impact on local environments. Key words for development workers in the late twentieth century are thus: *employment, environment, social equality,* and *sustainability.* These suggest some general guidelines which might help in determining what functions or skills are appropriate objectives for literacy in any particular project.

Some practical examples of functionality

Literacy and civil rights in Bangladesh

Gono Shahajjo Sangstha (an Oxfam-funded organisation) provides a good example of literacy promoted for a particular purpose: in this case to enable some of Bangladesh's poorest communities to fight injustice and to campaign for their rights. For example, it is easy for moneylenders to cheat non-literate peasants and to demand excessive repayments on small loans. One widow's story is typical: she had been obliged to mortgage her one acre of land for 1,000 taka when the crop failed. But when she came to pay back the money-lender and reclaim the deeds to

Bangladesh: a village group in northern Khulna, organised by Gono Shahajjo Sangstha, which combines functional literacy with social action. 'The Union Chairman distributes all the food aid to his friends. That's how he wins votes at the elections.'
Photo: John Clark

her land, he had forged the papers, and was demanding 20,000 taka. Her village group took the money-lender to court.

Literacy classes in this area of south-west Bangladesh often lead to the formation of village groups to deal with locally identified problems. An Oxfam report noted:

In one area a mass protest of 7,000 people, 1,500 of them women, forced local officials to remove a 'tax' on fishing in streams and canals which they had illegally imposed. Several other groups exposed local corruption in the government flood-relief programme: ration cards and emergency clothing supplies had gone missing, 'food-for-work' wages had not been properly paid in the emergency employment programmes. A number of groups were fighting for possession of khas, or government-owned land, to which they were entitled as landless labourers.

In circumstances like these, the need for literacy may well come after a social movement for change has taken root, leading to a demand for the empowerment of individuals and groups which literacy can bring.

Numeracy and income generation in Tanzania

Maasai villagers of Naisinyai in Tanzania set up their own health committee and organised classes at the church. In community discussions, people identified shortage of milk as a major problem: more than half their calves were dying from East Coast Fever. The men wanted to spray the cattle; the women preferred to build a cattle dip, which would use fewer chemicals. The committee held a vote, and the view of the women prevailed. Oxfam provided the building materials, and a loan for the first consignment of chemicals.

The women charge five Tanzanian shillings for each cow that goes through the dip. The village council decreed that all the cattle must be dipped once a week; herders from other villages brought their livestock too, until about 1,000 animals were going through the dip each day. East Coast Fever was virtually eradicated. The scheme started to make a profit. The loan was paid off, and the women began to look for ways of investing the income. They decided that their priority would be a borehole to provide clean drinking water, and pipes to deliver it round the village.

At first the women took turns to take home the day's takings for safe keeping. But too often the woman who carried the money-bag would come under pressure from her husband to lend him the money. For a time, every woman would carry a bag home every night, so that no one would know who really had the money. Before long, they realised that they needed to open a bank account. This meant organising numeracy classes, learning to sign their names and fill in forms. Eventually they progressed to book-keeping classes, with the help of an Oxfam health worker.

The group's next priority is to build and equip a village dispensary.

Some general guidelines on making literacy functional

- The purposes, both of the learners and of the promoting agencies, should be made clear to everyone. If they do not coincide, further discussion is essential.

- Learners do not think about their own development in separate 'sectors' (such as health, agriculture, or education), so literacy projects should be planned and thought about in an integrated way ('cross-sectorally', to use the jargon of development).

- People know why and when they need literacy skills. Programmes should be designed with them — and, where possible, by them.

- Any new developments need to be built on local ideas and local cultural practices, rather than models imported from somewhere else.

PART TWO

Planning for Literacy

Dakar, Senegal: a women's literacy group, run by PROFEMU, a local NGO.
'Why did you decide to attend literacy classes?' 'I wanted to know how to write my
language. It means that you can write your secrets. It helps you to open your mind, it
helps you to obtain other skills, and it helps you to recognise everything around.'
Photo: James Hawkins

CHAPTER 2

Recognising and assessing needs

This chapter examines in more detail the four key questions for planners outlined in the Preface.

- Who needs literacy?
- What do they need it for?
- What kind of literacy do they need?
- How will the programme be planned and implemented?

It follows the four general guidelines outlined at the end of the previous chapter. These imply that action should not be taken until the intended learners and the planners have discussed the proposed project in detail, and reached an agreement about what the community needs.

While some literacy projects are started in response to demand (what people say they want), the need for other projects is not always immediately obvious. As we have seen, other aspects of development, like providing clean water, may seem to be of more immediate importance and may take priority. Often, an agreed need for literacy emerges out of dialogue between development workers and local communities. Frequently, it is when people's lives change, or when change is introduced, that a productive dialogue about literacy can begin. Figure 2.1 shows how literacy might be useful in projects concerned with legal rights, employment, health, credit, and education.

Figure 2.1: Some areas of community development where literacy might be needed

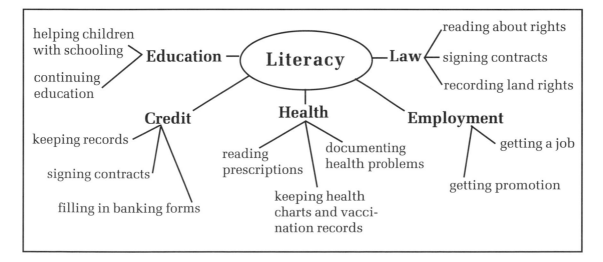

Asking the first questions

Before introducing new literacy skills into a community, it is important to understand how people have coped up till now, and in what ways reading, writing, and numeracy might help them to do things better. In every society, there exist traditional practices which, although they may not involve reading and writing, serve to record, assess, or communicate information. They may consist of cutting notches on tally sticks, stringing up coloured beads, or measuring by hand or eye. Any new literacy programme will be more meaningful to learners if it is based on existing practices, and such a programme is more likely to be sustainable than one based on entirely alien concepts.

An informal local survey could be conducted with a cross-section of the community. Questions might include the following.

- Have you ever thought about learning to read or write?
- If the answer is 'yes': what made you think about it?
- If the answer is 'no': can you think of any reason why knowing how to read might help you?
- Can you think of any particular situations where being able to read things would make a big difference to you?
- How have you dealt with situations like those in the past?
- Is there anything written down that you are able to recognise and understand at the moment?

Responses to a local survey will indicate not only whether people want literacy, but the type of literacy that is appropriate, and the different needs of young and old, men and women, workers and farmers.

Ways of assessing needs

These first questions are a good way of starting to assess the kind of literacy programme to be introduced into an area; and what methods to use. A more thorough survey of local practices and attitudes, looking at how people carry out everyday tasks, will give a more complete picture of what is happening now. A good education programme is one that is based on what people already know, and is aimed at what people need to know in the future. Time spent analysing this in advance will help to create an appropriate and sustainable programme, acceptable to the intended learners.

Who should ask questions

A survey can be carried out by 'insiders' — people who live in the area and may become learners in a programme — or by 'outsiders' — students or volunteers from another village, another town, or another country who have some experience in asking questions and may become teachers or group leaders in a programme.

Insiders know the area, and are known by the people they will be talking to; they speak the local language, and they know whom to ask. Involving them will give them some power in designing the programme they want. But will they be objective in their questions? Do they have a personal bias? Will they become drawn into local politics and serve the needs of the powerful rather than the poor?

Outsiders may not know the area or the people, and may be viewed with suspicion. If questions are asked through interpreters, the emphasis may be changed or simplified. It is often hard for interpreters to convey the feelings of the people concerned. And they, like insiders, will have their own (albeit different) biases.

Other surveys may already have been carried out in the area; if they give a general picture of the social or political situation, they may be worth consulting first.

Things to take into account before starting a survey

- Do you want an objective, distanced view of the situation?
- Do you want a more subjective view from people involved?
- Do women need to talk to other women? Should men be interviewed by other men?
- Are the interviewers sensitive to the needs of the people whom they interview?
- Will interpreters translate, unedited, exactly what is said, rather than what they think you want to hear?

How to ask questions

A survey will probably consist of asking a number of previously prepared questions which seem likely to gain the information needed. Questions should be asked informally, and not necessarily always in the same order. A rigid, formal interviewing process is unlikely to produce honest and open responses. You have to be prepared to talk about the insiders' interests, as well as the topics on your own check-list. (Researchers often call this a 'semi-structured interview'.) Interviews should be carried out with a cross-section of the people you wish to work with, taking into account things like age, sex, occupation, and perhaps status and income. People can be questioned individually or in groups, but the purpose of the survey needs to be explained thoroughly in advance, and you must ask their permission. The interview should appear relaxed and informal, giving people a chance to talk at some length, and giving the interviewer time to pursue ideas that come up. But essential questions and areas for discussion need to be fixed beforehand, and should form the overall structure of the interview. And, of course, the answers must be carefully recorded for future analysis and use in the planning process.

What sorts of question?

Questions should cover a community's existing practices, people's changing needs, their expectations of literacy, types of literacy which might be appropriate, and people's long-term goals.

Before a programme can be planned, you also need to ask questions about organisational matters, such as:

- the timing of classes;
- attitudes towards teachers;
- the best composition of classes (all ages together? men and women together?);
- the location of classes;
- the materials available;
- and existing literacy skills.

Most of the organisational issues can be checked out through simple 'yes/no' questions. For example, *Do you work in the home? Do you work in the evening? Can you arrive at the centre early in the morning?* Exploring attitudes will require longer, open-ended questions that encourage people to talk at length. For example, *In what situations do you feel you need to be able to read?*

Survey exercises with groups

Questionnaires are generally used with individuals, but group discussions are also a very useful and valuable way of finding out the particular needs of people in any community. In some cases they are more effective. Listening to ideas expressed by one person in a group can often generate new ideas in others. The process of discussion helps people to think through their own ideas, explain them to others, and consider them from different angles.

Brain-storming in a group can be very productive; the process is described in Chapter 3. However, in the early stages of discussion, people may need time to think through such matters as where or how a class might take place, or the topics they would like to cover in it. It might be helpful to represent the options visually, perhaps by using sticks, stones, or shells placed on the ground, or by drawing maps on paper or in the sand. The very process of representing an abstract idea with a concrete object is itself a literacy practice, and it gives the planner a chance to see whether learners are familiar with doing this, and to learn about the conventions which they normally use.

For example, when deciding on the best place to locate a literacy class, local people could be asked to make a rough sketch map of the area, perhaps using objects to represent the various features. With sticks to represent trees, and stones to represent buildings, the map will show how far each learner would have to walk from home to the possible sites for a centre.

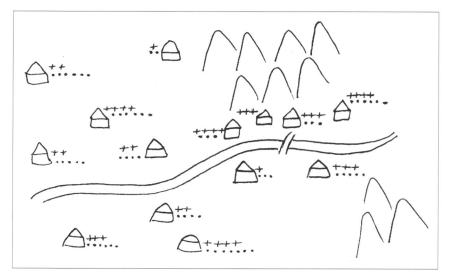

Figure 2.2: Representation of a village map drawn in the sand, showing hills, river, bridge, houses, and numbers of adults (+) and children (•) in each house. (Based on examples supplied by ACTIONAID, Uganda)

In the same way, when discussing literacy needs, stones or shells can be used to represent the different stages in cultivating, harvesting, storing, milling, and selling grain. Groups can begin to identify the particular difficulties encountered at different stages in the process, and the points at which literacy might help them. These might be calculating by weight instead of by volume; checking the price charged by the miller for the total amount of grain; or keeping records in order to decide in advance the most profitable time to sell.

When deciding priorities for literacy, stones or beads of different shapes can be used for the various literacy practices which the group might tackle, such as signing their names, opening a bank account, or recognising bus numbers. Individuals who have decided to learn in a group might like to sort out their own priorities first, before taking part in a group discussion.

Most cultures have a way of representing concepts visually. Some people record quantities by tying knots in cloth; others use numbers of beads or different-coloured beads to represent time passing, or the status of an individual. Tally sticks record quantities by notches cut in a piece of wood; totem poles represent more spiritual or abstract ideas. Some people prefer to have things represented visually: it helps them to analyse ideas into different components and grasp new concepts; others find it difficult to relate to two-dimensional images. In the same way, some readers will find it easier than others to relate to the diagrams used in this book. While these preferences may be partly determined by culture, they will also be due to individual learning styles.

Getting a group to talk about their needs without any indication of what is available or possible is generally difficult. Most people find it easier to make choices or express their feelings within clearly stated boundaries. In many cases, planners may need to define what these are, before asking a group to discuss their priorities. Again, stones, sticks, or

*Namibia: a ranking
exercise, using stones
and soft-drink cans*
Photo: Roger Yates

shells can be placed on the ground during a discussion, to represent what the planners feel they can offer.

Asking people to talk about priorities reveals the relative importance that they attach to various options. It is often a more effective way of making a decision than asking simple yes/no questions. Even when it is possible to choose only one of a number of options, a prioritising exercise can help a group to decide on the option that most people regard as the most important. For example, beads of different colours can be used to represent different days of the week, or times of day. If nine members of a group of twelve people prefer to meet on a Monday, but all of the group name Tuesday as either first or second choice, Tuesday may be the better option. The following exercises are, similarly, useful ways of identifying key features of a community's life and its literacy needs.

Seasonal calendars

Seasonal calendars record not only months or dates in a year, but the activities and problems that a community faces during a given period. They can be drawn up in advance by planners as they begin to work in an unfamiliar area. They are an important means of recording local knowledge and information, so local people should be involved in developing them.

As a literacy practice, making a calendar can form the focus of activity for early meetings with a group. The information it generates will be useful when designing an appropriate literacy programme. The process of compiling it also provides the chance to discuss with the community their familiarity with the idea of calendars, and the different conventions used for recording events.

A community calendar gives an overall picture of the workloads of various people in a community at different times of the year. Many communities, particularly in agricultural areas, have busy periods and slack periods, depending on the season. An educational programme should take this into account. Classes should be planned for a period of the year when people have the time and the energy to attend.

The content of the classes can be planned around the activities that are being undertaken by the community. For example, during sowing time, discussions might focus on the relative merits of new farming techniques for preparing the ground, or the choice of new varieties. Number work might be based on counting the number of rows or the total amount of seed needed, or calculating the risks when choosing new yields.

The type of information recorded on a seasonal calendar will vary according to the activities of the community. An urban group will not be affected by agricultural seasons in the same way, but are likely to have other patterns of busy and slack periods in their year, as well as different literacy needs at different times. Religious ceremonies often form significant points in people's memories, and can be used to cross-check dates and events. Once a community calendar has been drawn up, individuals can be given a copy on which to add their own dates and events.

Information recorded on seasonal calendars could include:

- ploughing, planting, weeding, and harvesting times for different crops;
- approximate times for applying fertiliser to different crops;
- periods of rainfall;
- expected temperatures;
- expected pests;
- periods when certain animal diseases are prevalent, and the need for special precautions;

Figure 2.3:
An example of a
seasonal calendar

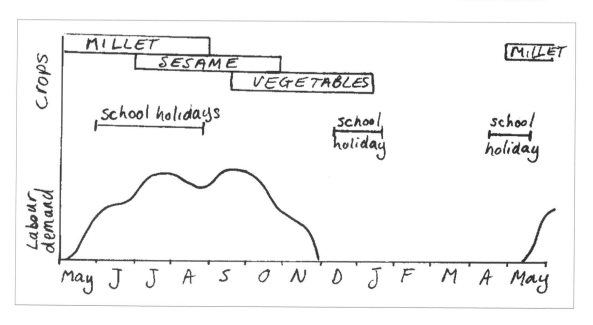

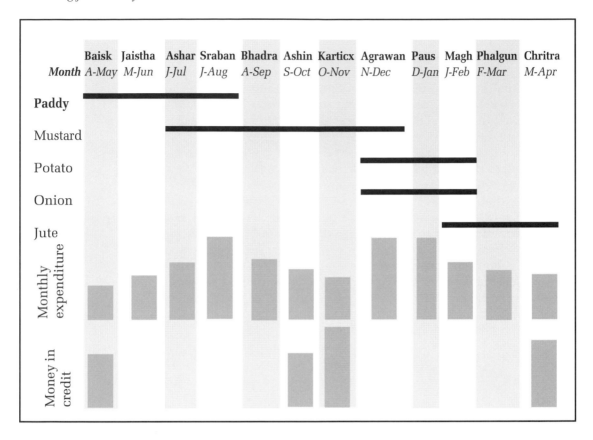

Figure 2.4:
Another example of a
seasonal calendar

- periods when human illness is common, and the need for preventative treatment;
- the demand for labour for different members of the family;
- school terms and holidays;
- religious ceremonies;
- public holidays.

Daily calendars can also be compiled and used to indicate the times of day when people may not be available for study. They can also be used to analyse and compare the work loads of different family members.

Time lines
In discussing changes in people's lives that have brought about the need for literacy, a time line drawn on paper or in the sand can help to put past events in sequence.

This is a good exercise to generate group discussion, as people recall the order in which various events occurred and mark them out along a straight line. By continuing the line on from the present to represent the future, people can be encouraged to indicate their expectations of literacy, the changes they anticipate, and the length of time they expect to be involved.

Local histories that begin to emerge through the construction of time lines should be noted and kept in mind. Later they can be recorded as reading material for subsequent literacy groups or for post-basic classes. Exercises involving time lines have been particularly successful with elders. A simple time line might look like Figure 2.5.

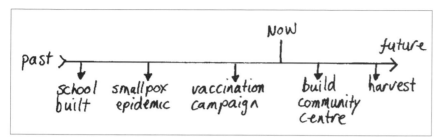

Figure 2.5:
A simple time line

With this and all the activities described above, care should be taken to ensure that people understand the exercise before they begin. Beware of giving too much information or of prompting people to reply in a certain way. They need to be given time and space to indicate their own priorities and make their own choices. Without this, a survey will be biased by the researcher and not give a true picture of the situation.

Who needs literacy?

The answer to this question will depend on the results of your survey. However, in terms of general development priorities, the focus of a literacy project is likely to be similar to the target of other development activities, like 'the poorest of the poor', or unemployed youth, or farmers who may be involved in a new agricultural programme. But the needs and interests of women always require special consideration. While women comprise at least half the world's population, only in parts of Latin America and the Caribbean is there anything approaching an equal balance between men and women in terms of literacy skills.

Recognising the needs of women

In recent years, development workers have become more aware of the often very different needs of groups of men and groups of women. Studies have shown the importance of seeing women as a separate group, and of making time to consider their special ways of living, working, speaking, and communicating.

Some facts
• Women in many areas of the world do a large part of the work in the home, within the family, in the fields, and in the market-place. The amount of time available to them for learning literacy is severely limited. There is a danger that literacy programmes and their outcomes will mean even more work for women.

- There are more literate men in the world than literate women: probably 20 per cent more.

- Formal schooling for boys has traditionally been seen as more important than formal schooling for girls.

- Most adult literacy programmes, in countries of the North and the South, attract more female students than male. In spite of pressures on their time, women do appear to want literacy.

In countries where women have little power, and there are high demands on their time, it is all the more important to identify their needs clearly, and to design programmes to meet them.

Most, if not all, the fundamental questions outlined in the previous sections may need to be addressed separately to groups of women. And there are other extra factors to be taken into account when looking specifically at the needs of women.

Bangladesh:
a literacy class for
women pavement-
dwellers. For mothers
of small children,
there may be no such
thing as free time for
study.
Photo: Liz Clayton

In the Rupandehi Province of Nepal, Women Working Together for Change (WATCH) is a locally based organisation, funded by Oxfam, which was set up to build confidence and self-reliance among women. WATCH works in the villages with groups of 15-30 women. They earn money from ventures such as seedling nurseries and mushroom cultivation. WATCH provides interest-free loans of 1,000 rupees to the poorest families and encourages them to start small money-making enterprises. When the women start to organise themselves, the need for literacy and a broader post-basic education becomes clear, and literacy classes are established.

Kathleen Rockhill's study of Hispanic women attending literacy classes in New Mexico (USA) in the late 1980s showed a connection between gender, education, and domestic violence. Many of the women whom she interviewed said that their husbands or partners felt threatened by their going out to classes and tried to prevent them, sometimes forcibly, from doing so. This is not unusual: it occurs in different ways in many parts of the world. When one member of a family chooses to do something to improve her or his life chances, the dynamics of the family are invariably changed. [12]

Culture

Is it culturally acceptable for women to discuss their needs with men, or to be taught by men? Are there women available to conduct initial surveys and later to act as teachers or as positive role-models? Will the women prefer to be questioned individually or as a group? In many parts of the world, men object to their wives and daughters becoming involved in educational programmes, which are sometimes the cause of domestic violence. Are women able to express their needs freely? Will they be able to attend classes, if necessary in secret? What would be the consequences for them?

Related to this is the equally important question of whether women should teach men, and the question of whether or not women and men should or can learn together in any particular cultural context. These questions are discussed in Chapter 4.

Confidence

Do the women of the community have the confidence to attend literacy classes? Have they always seen literacy as a male preserve? Do they see it as something that might be available and useful to women? Do existing attitudes need to be challenged?

Changes

Are there social or domestic changes that have affected or will affect women's need for literacy, such as a tendency for men to migrate to the towns, leaving rural women in charge of households and communicating with their partners by letter? Will these new roles lead to the need for further skills, such as training in management, or second-language literacy?

Test your own assumptions!

When making a survey of how women spend their time, and trying to assess their existing need for literacy, it is important not to ignore the possibility for change within the programme. Women often mention increased self-confidence as the most important outcome of their literacy programme. Programme planners often focus on the *content* of the programmes and the information that can be passed on. Many women's programmes have been designed to centre on issues of child-care or their domestic roles within the household. Do women want 'welfare' programmes that help them to complete their current tasks 'better'? Or do they want 'equity' programmes that will give them access to opportunities similar to those of the men of their community? Programmes which concentrate on domestic roles will do little to change the balance of power.

If women decide that they want to challenge their current roles, they will need to address the attitudes of the men in the community, and seek their co-operation. Issues of gender are not specifically a women's concern. Men will, in the same way, need to think about, understand, and question which tasks, powers, and privileges are distributed on the basis of gender, and where there is scope for change.

In trying to recognise the needs of women, it is easy to see them as a unified group who share the same needs. But, as with any group, there will be strong differences: differences between working women, single women, mothers, grandmothers, young women, and old women; and differences of class and caste and expectations. Has every woman been given the chance to express her needs? Have all the differences been taken into account?

When making a survey of certain groups, including women, it is important not to start from the assumption that they are inevitably marginalised, because this may not be the case. We need to ask:

- What strengths do women have?
- In what way are women's groups organised?
- What power do they traditionally hold?
- What assumptions have been made in advance about their roles?

It is also important not to begin with a culturally biased view of what women need. It is too easy for outsiders to adopt attitudes which reflect Western assumptions. Deciding whether to work within existing structures and roles or to challenge them can be done only by the users of a programme themselves, and in their own time. In order truly to recognise other people's needs, it is important to be free of any pre-conceived idea of what these may be.

Development workers should ask themselves all the time:

- What is actually happening now?
- What can we learn from it?
- What are the alternatives?
- Which of these alternatives do the users want?
- How do these relate to literacy?

Recognising age-related needs

In every community there will be groups with specific needs which need to be specially considered. Any survey of the needs of a community must take care to identify what these groups might be: homeless people, for

Older people often prefer to learn with people in the same age-group — as here, in a literacy class for grandmothers in La Paz, Bolivia.
Photo: Jenny Matthews

instance; the unemployed; migrant workers; elderly people; or refugee groups. Once they have been identified, it may be possible to make provision to include them within new developments, or to set up something specifically for them. Programmes which aim to introduce change into a community need to take into account all groups within that community, considering both their own particular needs and the ways in which they will be affected by change in other areas.

People's needs for literacy, the types of skill they require, and the way they are best able to acquire them will not remain constant throughout their lives. As people grow and mature, their needs will change. In the past, some cultures saw learning as something that happened in the early part of life: in particular, childhood was seen as the only time for formal schooling; but this view is now questioned. People have always taken on different responsibilities at different stages of their lives, but they may have been prepared for these roles by older members of the family or community. Now, changes in technology and in community life often mean that young adults need to learn things which older people may not know about. Rapid changes in technology and in community life are all contributing to a situation where new skills, new ideas, and new technology demand continuing re-education, learning, and unlearning throughout life. It is no longer the case that the learning which takes place in the early part of life will be sufficient to carry someone through to old age.

While some forms of learning and education may be appropriate to all members of a community, there are times when people will want to learn with members of their own age-group. The topics they want to discuss and the skills they need will be different from those that are of concern to a person older or younger than themselves. Being with people of a similar age-group and situation in life can help to strengthen individual self-awareness, in terms of what individuals need to learn and also in terms of what they have to offer. Moreover, people of different ages often have different learning styles.

We do not advocate constant segregation by age in literacy learning. Being with people of different ages can help to improve communication and understanding between them. There may be times for integrated, all-age groups and times for separate groups. However, planners and development workers do need to take age into account. Literacy workers should be made aware of age-related needs and, as with all groups, be encouraged to identify with the life situation of the people with whom they are working.

In some African cultures a person's age-group is particularly important. At certain stages in their lives such as circumcision and the onset of puberty, young people spend time with their peers, away from most adults, learning about their new roles and responsibilities. In Senegal at such a time, a group of young people formed their own drama group. They wanted to take an active role in development issues and particularly to let people know about the problems that would be created by the government's decision to build a dam and flood arable land. They wrote a play and travelled together round local villages, performing it and discussing the issues with the villagers.

A changing view of elders

Traditionally in countries of the South, age has been seen to bring increased wisdom and knowledge. Elders in most communities have held power and commanded respect. This is beginning to change, particularly in areas which are undergoing rapid development. Young people often feel that they are more in touch with the new world than their elders are. Young people now command more power, and older people are increasingly seen as having little to offer. This Western view of elders as frail or needy is in danger of spreading throughout the developing world.

Increased poverty in many of the already poorer countries has added to the strain on extended families and has affected traditional family structures. Migration to find paid work in the cities has taken younger people away from family homes. Elders in many countries are often living alone and seen as out of touch.

Marginalising elders and assuming that they have little to offer prevents their full participation within a community. Literacy and education programmes are too often seen as something for the young. Many planners feel that literacy programmes should be aimed at those who are economically productive, and they assume that elders do not fall

A group of older people in the Windward Islands were questioned about what they wanted from a literacy programme. One of their priorities was to record some of their knowledge, which younger people no longer seemed interested in. In particular they wanted to write down events that had happened throughout their lifetime, and record some of the plant medicines and natural remedies which they and their families had always used. They felt that when the new enthusiasm for modern medicine had subsided, people would again want to use some of the traditional remedies.

into this group. But it is a mistake to see the young as the only economically productive group. Older people often have the time and the wisdom to work in a variety of ways, particularly in the administrative tasks and other support roles that are needed in literacy programmes. Their time and their wisdom can be of positive value to the rest of the community, if they are given the opportunity to use them.

In many areas, with increased demands on younger women's time, it is grandmothers and elders who are responsible for bringing up children. They play a vital economic role here, as well as having a direct influence on the welfare and attitudes of young children.

Before introducing change into a community, it is important to remember that elders will have seen and lived through many other sorts of change before. Whatever is new in current ideas about development, it is the *process* of change, and its effect on community life, that they will have experienced in the past. Their understanding and support can be invaluable.

Some facts

- The world's population is growing older. The number of older people in the developing world is growing particularly fast. It is expected to increase by more than 80 per cent between 1980 and the year 2000.

- When older people are left to care for children, their influence in encouraging children to read is as great as that claimed for mothers.

- Short-term memory generally becomes worse as people grow older; long-term memory improves.

- Older adults bring knowledge and experience of life to learning, which is an advantage when acquiring new information and skills.

- Research shows that, if people continue to use their brains, effective learning can continue well into old age.

- Age is a cultural construct. In some communities, people are considered old at 35; in others they are not seen as 'middle-aged' until they are over 40.

71764

Planning work with different age-groups

What particular needs will each group have?

- Children have a lot of energy and may want to move around and be active in their classes. Older people may prefer to be more reflective and spend more time in discussion.

- Eye-sight usually deteriorates with age (although people of all ages may have difficulties in seeing clearly). Ensure good lighting, and hold classes in daylight hours, if possible. Where appropriate, test to see whether spectacles are needed.

- How will you plan the different daily programmes of each age-group? Will one group be excluded from coming to a class if it is set at a certain time?

- What particular interests will each group have? What topics will they want to discuss? What materials will they be interested in reading? What examples will they identify with?

- How will the aims and needs of each age-group differ? Think about children, teenagers, adults, elders. How do their responsibilities change at different stages of their lives, and how will this affect their literacy needs?

- Will the understanding of different groups of people be increased by including them in one learning group? Are there particular cultural difficulties in their learning together? If people are to be put into groups, is sex a better criterion than age?

- How will learners feel about a literacy worker from a different age-group? Older people may find it difficult to be taught by a younger person, who may in turn find it difficult to be in a position of teaching elders. Young people may be able to relate better to someone who is not much older than themselves.

- How can the skills of each particular age-group be harnessed and used positively? What in particular do they have to contribute to, as well as gain from, the whole community?

- What does each group really think about people older and younger than themselves? Is their view an accurate one? Can a literacy or learning group contribute to a better understanding between generations, as well as sharpening a generation's view of its own abilities?

Again, it is generally the local people themselves who will be in the best position to answer these questions. Care should be taken to consult with people from all age-groups when planning a programme.

CHAPTER 3

Looking at literacies and establishing aims

If you are asked to provide training in literacy skills, what kind of literacy should you offer? The safest answer is that, once you have gone though the processes of discussion outlined in the previous chapter, you should be guided by what the learners say they want and can be shown to need. When in doubt, remember that the learners know best, for attendance at literacy classes is usually a voluntary activity, and the importance of learners' motivation should never be underestimated. One difficult and often contentious issue is the question of language choice.

Language choice: long-term and short-term needs

While it is generally accepted that people acquire literacy best in their mother-tongue, it is also true there is very little written material available in a large number of principally oral languages. Learning to read and write in a local language which has very restricted use may soon become frustrating for learners. However, if the need for literacy is related to carrying out a relatively small and locally based task, acquiring literacy in a second language may not be necessary. Obviously, the needs of different groups will vary, but introducing different literacies or different languages within one community may restrict the use and value of what is learned. In discussing literacy needs with a community, it is important to take both a short-term and a long-term view of what should be done. What are the tasks which the community may want to carry out almost immediately, and what 'post-basic' or continuing education programmes might they wish to move on to in the future?

Language choice will ultimately be based on people's reasons for wanting to become literate and the goals they set themselves. In areas where they live surrounded by newspapers, advertisements, messages, and signs, there are often strong reasons for wanting to become literate in the dominant language. This could be referred to as 'the language of first sight', just as the mother-tongue is 'the language of first hearing'.

In helping people to decide the language they will choose for literacy, it is useful to understand the power-related implications behind that choice.

In the Oxfam-funded Bulamahlo learning project, in a black settlement called Shiluvane, in the Transvaal, South Africa, people are learning to read and write in Sotho, the vernacular (local) language of the area. The number of books and other reading materials in Sotho is limited, but for many of the learners the aim in becoming literate is to correspond with members of their family who are spread throughout South Africa. One woman, typical of many, reported: 'Sometimes my husband sends me money, and I didn't know how to sign for it at the Post Office. And when he wrote letters, I had to ask friends to read them for me. They know all my secrets. Sometimes I even had to pay people to sign for my money or read my letters.' It is the policy of many South African programmes for people to learn to read and write initially in their first language, and then to progress to English if they need it for work. The same woman reported: 'I worked in a white farmer's house for six years. If I answered the phone when no one was at home, I could never take a message, because I couldn't write. I couldn't even write down the phone number.' Now her ambition is to become a teacher, 'to share all this cleverness with others'.

South Africa: an open-air class run by the Bulamahlo Learning Project in Shiluvane, Transvaal. Each student has three two-hour classes each week.

Photo: Matthew Sherrington

- Language is often the most important basis for a sense of individual, cultural, and political identity.

- Where the language of education is different from that of the home, home life may be seen as inferior to social spheres where knowledge and learning mean power.

- People may be deterred from entering education because they have a limited knowledge of the language taught.

- People who speak and write the dominant language will have better access to information and therefore to power.

- When a language is written down, it assumes authority and tends to become standardised. Other forms of that language, such as dialects and creoles, may then be seen as less important. As a result, people who speak dialects and creoles may be at a disadvantage.

- While a country may have decided upon its own national language, the former colonial language may still dominate and be understood as 'the language of power', as with English in many former British colonies. In India, where Hindi is the national language, English is still widely spoken in government, politics, industry, and education. The language issue in such a large country is further complicated by the fact that in many parts of the south there is little understanding of Hindi, and English tends to be used as a *lingua franca* instead.

- Of the 4,000 languages spoken in the world, only 300 are in regular use in their written form, and fewer than 100 have a significant written literature.

- Some minority languages may consist of only a few thousand speakers.

- There is often a wide regional variation in the script and writing conventions of local languages. Literacy programmes in one area may differ significantly from those in another, and communication between areas may therefore be restricted.

- Many languages are in danger of dying out. (It has been estimated that 50 per cent of the languages of the world will disappear within a lifetime.) *Teaching* literacy in an endangered language can help to increase its value and extend its usage. *Learning* literacy in an endangered language often has limited use.

- Materials available in local languages will be restricted. People may be able to read only what they have written for themselves, or what has been specially written for them. Locally produced materials are rarely, if ever, financially viable.

- Schools often begin with teaching literacy in the mother-tongue and move on to the dominant language in later years. There is no firm evidence to suggest that second-language literacy is eventually helped or hindered by a two-step approach.

The choice of language for literacy is a crucial one and needs to decided at local level. It should take into account both the long-term and the short-term needs of learners, the available materials and financial resources, national policy, and the status of the languages in question. Its significance should not be underestimated.

[In Senegal, most literacy programmes are in the learners' first language, while all formal education is in French.]

What is now beginning to happen in Senegal might be compared to the days in Europe when literacy passed from the language of the educated elite (Latin and Greek) into national language education (in German, French, English ...), which eventually reached the majority of the population.

The formal Senegalese system of education in French is sometimes referred to as 'imported knowledge'. Adding imported knowledge to an already sound basic-skill level, to high self-esteem, and to an 'indigenous' knowledge base which is highly valorised is an invaluable step towards growth, change, and development.

But if imported knowledge is supposed to give or replace these skills, self-esteem, and knowledge base, it can have disastrous effects on the perceptions and abilities of learners. In this context, learners become passive recipients of 'messages' sent from 'outside', and this passivity (and the resulting confusion) makes true learning, independence, and subsequent action impossible.[13]

What is the programme for?

As we have seen, answers to the question *What kind of literacy?* are closely bound up with the aims of the learners. It is becoming clear that the four key questions for planners cannot be considered in isolation. In real life they are all mixed up together. We shall return to this problem later.

Establishing aims

Before beginning to plan literacy training, whether for individuals or groups, it is important that everyone is clear and in agreement on the programme's overall aims or purposes. What a programme intends to achieve will greatly affect how a programme is planned and taught. After the needs of the various groups have been assessed, the people who will be involved in learning need to agree on a set of common aims.

Learners should play a large part in setting the aims for their own programmes. If aims are set for them by outsiders, there is a big risk that they will either be irrelevant, or that they will not satisfy what the learners feel they themselves need at that time. In the first case, everyone's time is wasted; in the second, it is hard for learners to be motivated, unless they recognise that what they are learning is useful.

However, we should not underestimate the contribution of planners or literacy workers: they also have a role to play. The learners' experience is necessarily limited, and someone from outside may be able to offer ideas which the group would not have thought of themselves. A VSO volunteer working in Islamabad, for example, found a group of adults basing aims for their course on a primary-school curriculum. They had no direct experience of adult approaches to classroom learning. While they recognised that they were learning, as adults, every day of their lives, they associated literacy with being in the classroom, being taught, and 'going back to school'. Acquiring literacy skills was for them a very passive experience, and, not surprisingly, the drop-out rate was high.

In establishing aims, a brain-storming exercise may be a good starting point. Brain-storming is an activity that generates a lot of energy, and is often a useful way to gather ideas. It means encouraging everyone in the group to contribute any ideas that occur to them, without thinking critically about them. Some ideas will be useful; others may be inappropriate, but these will often spark off new, more relevant ideas in other people's minds. For this reason it is better for the literacy worker to accept all suggestions without comment or judgement, recording everything that is offered.

Initially it is a light-hearted exercise. The serious work begins when the group has run out of ideas. All the suggestions are then discussed, and those that are not generally felt to be relevant are rejected. The rest are grouped together, or placed in order of importance or complexity. Gradually, the suggestions are turned into aims for a learning programme, and an outline of how they should be tackled. If a chalk-board is used to record the results of a brain-storming exercise, the result may look something like Figure 3.1: aims are written down, some are later crossed out, and some are grouped. But you should bear in mind that new learners may not be able to interpret a relatively complex arrangement of words like this. They will need to find other ways of recording and remembering the suggestions made; see *Survey exercises with groups* in Chapter 2.

Remember that it is the *process* of agreeing aims which is important. A trainer may well have an overview, and suggest ideas which the group itself may not have thought of. Part of the trainer's role is to extend the learners' knowledge and ideas. But it is easy for trainers, planning on their own, to make misguided assumptions about a group and choose aims which are inappropriate to the learners.

Although it is often easier to begin teaching with a primer or work book, materials prepared in advance are generally based on the aims of an outsider. People in different situations will have their own ideas and their own aims. While they may decide to use a primer that has been produced on a large scale, it will be more successful if it is used selectively to serve the aims decided by the learners.

Remember that people's aims will change and grow as they learn more, but certain overall aims need to be established in advance. If you don't know where you are going, it is very difficult to get there!

Skills and themes

Overall aims for learning will probably include a number of skills and themes: things that people want to learn to do, and things that people want to learn about. These themes and skills will arise out of the early discussions undertaken to assess the community's needs, and may be agreed upon during the first meeting of a group.

Target skills may include:

- writing and signing one's name
- writing down addresses
- reading the Bible, the Koran, or other scriptures
- writing a personal letter
- understanding a business contract
- keeping records
- recognising road signs
- helping children with school-work
- reading a newspaper.

Key themes may include:

- the use of banks
- improved nutrition
- how a co-operative works
- crop diseases
- legal rights
- electricity and safety
- the history of political change.

Deciding on themes and skills will help to determine what is to be learned and in what order. When working with a group, every member of the group should be given an opportunity to express personal aims before deciding which ones are shared, and establishing common priorities. Themes and skills will probably be taught alongside each other, and will involve the writing and number work that is necessary for confidence in each of these areas.

In establishing aims, remember:

- If the learning is to be useful, the aims should be decided on in consultation with the learners themselves, and not by outsiders alone.

- Aims should be analysed and clarified. For example, in looking at the history of political change, what sorts of change do people want to know about? What is it that they want to understand? The aims which people set themselves have to be within their grasp, so that they are able to reach them and feel they are making progress.

- Although aims need to be established in advance, they may well change and will need to be reviewed regularly.

Establishing aims for a learning programme will help individuals to decide whether they want to be involved. It will help the person planning the course to decide who should teach what. One person need not be responsible for teaching everything. There will be many themes which members of the group know far more about than the literacy worker does. When an outline programme has been drawn up, planners can begin to consider how it might best be organised.

CHAPTER 4

Getting organised: some practical issues

In this chapter we will consider practical issues: how often the group should meet; what time of year and day the classes should be held; where groups should meet; how big the classes should be; whether women and men should learn together; drawing up a programme; involving other people; and planning for assessment and evaluation. Part Three will consider classroom practice in much more detail.

When and how often should the group meet?

When planning a programme of learning, with an individual, a group, or a series of groups, it is important to decide on a time and a place to meet. However informal the class, meetings which are left to chance are too easily cancelled or overlooked. Regular meetings and regular practice are important in learning new skills. Classes should be planned in advance, bearing in mind the time of day and the time of year.

People attending literacy classes will need to fit them into the other activities in their lives. For farmers there are certain times of year when any extra activities are impossible. During planting and harvesting times, they may be working in the fields from early morning to late at night; while at other times of the year, for men at least, a large part of the day is free. Nomadic herders who travel with their livestock may be away for long periods at a time, but still spend two to three months in one place.

In a literacy programme in Senegal, classes were held twice a week for three hours. Learners worked for one and a half hours on numeracy, then for one and a half hours on literacy, following lessons set out in a primer. The language used was Pulaar, the first language of the area. It is a phonetic language, where each letter stands for a single sound, and there is a direct relationship between the sound of a word and the way it is written down. Some people were reading simple texts and writing letters after three months.

In India, female construction workers on a building site were unable to organise regular classes. They attended weekend workshops with a tutor about once every two months, and between workshops they used their lunch-times to work together on their books. The language used was Rajasthani, written in Hindi script. They were all living in a city where literacy was very much part of their environment. Some people progressed faster than others, but most of them could gain something from reading a newspaper after six months and four weekend workshops.

Although classes need to be fixed in advance, they need not involve the same amount of time week by week. The group may decide to meet once, twice, or three times a week, or even daily for a short period. It is impossible to predict how much time is needed to acquire literacy skills. It depends on the skills that people want, the skills they start with, the writing system they will use, and other factors. But a one-month or two-month period with classes once, twice, or three times a week is long enough to make a significant start.

Fixing a time of day to meet means considering not only people's other tasks, and when they will be free, but also their energy levels. Early morning or mid-morning is often a good time for learning, when people are still fresh and the day is not too hot. However, this is also the time when people generally work in the fields or prepare the mid-day meal.

Mid-afternoon, after eating, may be a time when there are fewer outside demands, but energy levels are low and students may find themselves falling asleep in class.

During the cool of the evening, when the sun has gone down, may be a popular time for organising classes, but this means that artificial light must be provided. There is the cost of lamps and fuel to be considered, and interference from insects. Elders, or those with poor eyesight, generally find it more difficult to work by artificial light, which can cause eye strain.

In a literacy programme in Nepal, classes are held on four evenings a week for a period of six months. Each class generally lasts for two hours. Regular attendance means that many learners progress quickly and, by the end of six months, can write their names and recognise individual letters of the alphabet and most words, if written in large letters. However, VSO volunteers report that few learners are able to transfer these skills to real-life situations; they cannot read joined-up letters, newspaper headlines, or signboards. When asked about this, one woman replied: 'I am only able to read the literacy book. I do not have attention for those other things.' If they are not able to put their new skills to use, people who learn quickly and intensively may lose their skills just as fast.

Bangladesh: learning by the light of a paraffin lamp. People are usually more relaxed in the cool of the evening; but there is the cost of artificial light to be considered.

Photo: Ro Cole

There is no one ideal time for learning, but it may help to remember:

- Classes should be between one and two hours long. Less than one hour is often too short. It is hard to concentrate for more than two hours.

- There should be frequent changes of activity (see Chapter 7, 'Planning a session'). This is particularly good for keeping people awake and interested during times of low energy.

- Students should be involved and active. People used to manual work may find sitting down uncomfortable, whatever time of day it is. It is always easier for people to learn if they are active and involved.

- The timing of the classes should be decided with all the learners. They will know what time of day they are free and able to learn. But this may well depend on people's jobs, and also it may be different for men and women, for parents and for adults without child-care responsibilities.

Where should the group meet?

Agreeing on a place to meet means finding somewhere which can be reached by everyone; is sheltered from sun, wind, and rain; has space for everyone in the group to sit comfortably; and will leave people undisturbed by curious children or animals.

Many adult literacy groups meet in school buildings, after the children have finished using them. The advantages of a school are that it is generally seen as a place for studying; tables and chairs are often there already; and there is often a board and chalk. The disadvantages of a school are that adults may feel they are being treated as children and 'sent

In Johannesburg, the 'Centres of Concern' run adult literacy classes in the evenings. They are taught by volunteers and generally held in local primary schools. No fee is charged, whether or not the students are in paid employment.

As the schools are often in the centre of residential areas, they can be easily reached by everyone. Classrooms are already equipped with blackboard and chalk, desks and chairs. The volunteer teachers attend training courses on a regular basis, and are taught how to work with adult students.

However, some students were apprehensive about attending for the first time. They were afraid of being intimidated by the teacher and treated as if they were six or seven years old.

Other students attended and found that the classes were taught quite differently from anything they had experienced as school children. But in some cases their friends and family made fun of them and teased them about 'going back to school again'. This made some students all the more determined to succeed. Others felt humiliated by the teasing and left.

back to school'; tables and chairs may be the wrong size; and the unfamiliar environment may make students feel uncomfortable and unsure of themselves.

Sitting in rows behind desks is not the best way to learn. People who are more used to sitting on the ground and to holding meetings outside may not need tables, or even a building in which to study. When working with individuals or small groups, it may be easier to meet in someone's house.

Adult learners often feel ill at ease in the formal context of a school classroom — as here, perhaps, in a literacy class in Namibia.
Photo: Kelvin Jenkins

The size and structure of the group

There is no recommended minimum size of group. Some people learn best on their own with one teacher; others prefer to be in a group. The maximum number that will allow time for everyone to contribute and learn effectively with one teacher has been found to be around 15. Adult students generally prefer to sit in a circle, where everyone can see each other and be seen. This avoids creating the atmosphere of a school, where pupils sit in rows and the teacher stands at the front. It encourages everyone in the group to participate actively in the lessons. It takes away some of the feeling that the teacher is superior to or more powerful than the group members. When choosing a place for learning, there should be enough space for people to sit together in this way.

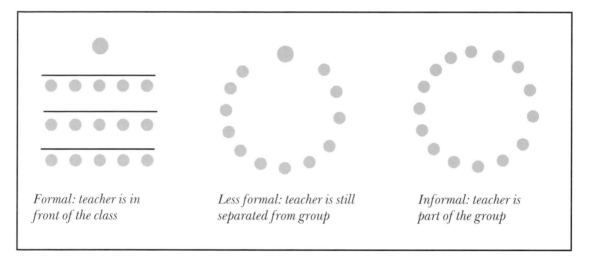

Formal: teacher is in front of the class

Less formal: teacher is still separated from group

Informal: teacher is part of the group

Figure 4.1:
Some alternative seating arrangements

Should men and women learn together?

This decision will depend on the local culture, and only the people who will be involved can decide. Some women prefer to be taught separately from men. Some cultures insist on divided classes. There will be other situations in which men and women prefer to be taught together, particularly when working for aims which benefit the whole community.

There is also the question of whether women should teach men. In the case of a literacy programme in Mali, there were more women volunteering to act as literacy workers than men. Most of them were very competent, but, in a Muslim culture, mixed classes or men-only classes would not be accustomed to seeing a woman in the role of teacher. The women teachers solved this problem by pairing up initially with male literacy workers, and presenting themselves in teams of two. During the first few visits, the male worker would take the lead, only gradually standing back and allowing the female worker to play a bigger role. In this way she was able slowly to gain the respect of the class. When she felt confident, the male worker would develop a 'diplomatic illness' that meant he was unable to come for the next few weeks. Provided that the classes continued to go well, he did not reappear, and moved on to work with another group. The Malian women felt that this approach, although it involved deception, was preferable to confronting the men and insisting that they should accept female teachers from the beginning. Instead they began by respecting the cultural conventions of the learners, and then working to earn their trust.

Drawing up a programme

Drawing up a programme for a course means matching the aims set by the group with the times set aside to work together. It will probably mean linking the themes with the skills they need, and introducing the writing and number work involved in these skills. This will give the learners and the group leader a rough idea of what they will be doing when.

It is difficult to predict in advance how long something will take. The group's priorities may change when the programme gets under way, and other areas of interest may emerge. Any programme will need to be modified as time goes by. But an overall programme for learning will help students to see how far they are progressing towards reaching their aims.

Involving other people

Planning and running a literacy programme, however small, will involve a number of people: in setting the aims and outlining the content for the course; in organising a place to meet; and in choosing a group leader. If the literacy programme is to be linked into other development activities, it is important to involve the people who work in them.

Development workers will be able to provide information on the importance of literacy to other development activities. Working closely with them will help a literacy worker to understand in more depth some of the things which learners need to do with literacy. The learners themselves will be able to give detailed information on some of these things. A planner who does not listen to the learners, or to other colleagues working with them, is in danger of focusing only on his or her own programme. *It is important that literacy is constantly seen in the context of people's lives.*

There are crucial questions to consider early in the planning stage.

- Who will act as teacher or leader of the literacy group?
- Will one person do all the teaching?
- Are there other development workers who could be involved in planning a programme?
- Are there others who could do part of the teaching, especially within their specialist areas like small-business management or agriculture?
- Are there members of the learning group who could do part of the teaching?

• Will the literacy workers be paid for their time, and how will the payments be funded?

On many topics, members of the group will have more experience or more knowledge to contribute than the literacy worker. Such members can be a useful resource, adding to discussions or even presenting a part of the session. They can be asked in advance to take over certain activities with the whole group, or to work as leaders of small groups.

Involving learners as teachers helps to establish the power *within* the group rather than outside it, and recognises and values the skills which learners already have. Care should be taken to involve everyone who wants to contribute.

In Chapter 8 we discuss the question of whether to involve outsiders to present specialist topics. Although we can give some general guidelines on issues to be taken into account, it should be remembered that all decisions must be made in the context of particular programmes. These decisions will depend on the people who are able to be involved, the work they will be asked to do, and the money that is available to pay them.

Planning for assessment and evaluation

It is important at the outset to think about assessment and evaluation. If you neglect to do this at the planning stage, you may find at the end of the course that you have not asked the questions which you might be required to answer, or kept the records which you might be required to produce. And you will have lost many opportunities for using assessment and evaluation as a valuable means of learning during the course.

Figure 4.2: Timetable for assessment and evaluation

In the beginning: Identify the purposes of assessment and evaluation and everybody's expectations of the programme
During the course: Learners' aims may alter; so may the aims and methods of the development workers
At the end: Review and reflect on learners' learning (anticipated and unanticipated)
Evaluation — some time later: How is the learning experience being used? What has been the impact?

Assessment and evaluation should take place, in one form or another, at all stages of a literacy programme. Figure 4.2 illustrates this. There are two main kinds of assessment, for which the technical terms are *formative* and *summative*. Assessment is called 'formative' when the outcomes are used to shape future practice and organisation. At the end of a course there is usually an evaluation; often this is required by the funding agencies. Such evaluation is called 'summative', because it provides a summary of what has happened and the outcomes of the programme. *Impact evaluation* is the term used for identifying the effects of a course on the lives of the learners. We will look at these in more detail in Chapter 9.

What do you want from assessment?

One way to start is to think about assessment and evaluation from the perspectives of those involved. Here we will consider the interests and requirements of learners, literacy workers, and the funding agency (though others, such as employers and the wider community, might also have an interest). Each of these parties should be asked the question: *'What do you want from assessment?'* This is a good way of introducing the topic of assessment and of encouraging involvement in the process.

Learners want to know how they are getting on: are they making good progress? **Literacy workers** are anxious to know that their teaching is on the right track: whether or not their methods are helping the learners. The **funding bodies** want to know that their money is being wisely spent: that the learners are achieving what they were supposed to achieve; and the **partner agency** needs to know that its organisational approach is working well. While many of these interests overlap, each party is likely to have some specific interests. For example, the funding agency will want the facts and figures about attendances and costs. Individual learners are unlikely to be interested in such statistics. It may be necessary to conduct different assessments/reviews to meet different needs; but, with a little creativity, it should be possible to use class records and other information more efficiently.

Three key points are worth bearing in mind when planning for assessments and evaluations.

1 *The outcomes of assessment and evaluation must be useful.* All too often, the results of assessment and reviews are not used constructively. There is no point in assessment if no one is going to take any notice of the outcomes. The results of assessment should be used to support learning and teaching, to improve the programme.

2 *The ways in which the programme is assessed and evaluated should be in sympathy with the values of the programme and the styles of teaching and learning that it will use.* Learner-centred, participatory approaches to learning and teaching should be matched with learner-centred, participatory approaches to assessment. In this way, assessment becomes an integral and supportive part of the learning. Being able to do this requires an attitude of mind, rather than a battery of tools. Chapter 9 suggests some imaginative ways of identifying, observing, and recognising change. Here we should simply note that there are other ways of measuring progress than by the conventional methods of *normed assessment* and *criterion-based assessment*, which are related either to other people's performance or to pre-determined criteria. *Ipsative assessment* is concerned with gauging the progress made by an individual in relation to his or her own personal starting-point. It compares what the person can do now with what he or she could do previously. It allows for individuals to progress at their own rate to develop the skills they need. Progress can be identified in terms of personal successes and achievements, rather than against set examinations or general expectations. It is a very useful mode of assessment for programmes that are not primarily concerned with formal accreditation.

3 *The processes of assessment and evaluation should not be a routine, mechanical chore*. Keeping records and assessing will become tedious, if the outcomes are not used and the information is not seen to be valued. Assessment and evaluation are about asking questions. Literacy workers should never stop asking questions about the methods and processes being used for assessment! Assessment and evaluation, when they are part of the learning process, are dynamic activities that will help to keep the learning moving easily and smoothly.

The process of assessment

Assessment is never neutral. It involves making many political and educational choices. The questions in Table 4.1 may help literacy workers, learners, and funding organisations to begin to develop a framework for assessment that fits in with their particular programme and will contribute to its success.

Keeping records

Having a set of useful records will help the assessing and reviewing process. With careful thought and planning, there is no need to become a slave to keeping records. We need to ask ourselves questions similar to those in Table 4.1. Why keep records? What will they be used for? What should we keep records of? How should they be kept? By whom? etc. This will help the worker and the learners to design ways of keeping records that will suit them.

It is useful to keep records of attendances. Irregular attendance will directly affect a person's learning. Attendance records may offer valuable information when an individual's progress is being discussed.

Keeping records of lesson plans, and noting down what actually happened during a session, or how particular materials were used, will help the worker to plan later sessions and keep track of how things are going.

As part of keeping records, learners can keep a diary, or a note of what they read, write, and calculate in their everyday lives (or of tasks which

Who is assessment for:
- the learner
- the development worker
- the programme providers
- the sponsor/funder/employer?

What is the purpose:
- to identify progress
- to check the appropriateness of teaching methods
- to boost confidence
- to find out what is not going well
- to record achievement
- to establish cost/benefits
- to find out what needs changing
- to check if the programme is on the right track
- to be able to make comparisons
- to gain a certificate or accreditation?

What to assess:
- skills learned
- concepts grasped
- understanding of ideas
- application of learning
- personal and social development

How to assess:
- formal/informal styles
- observation
- discussion
- tests/examinations (oral/paper and pencil/practical)
- assignments?

Who is to assess:
- development workers
- the learner (self)
- the learners (peers)
- the learner's family
- the learner's employer
- others?

How to record progress:
- grades/percentages/tick lists/grading scales
- written/recorded statements
- portfolio of work and comments?

How to interpret progress:
- norm-based assessment
- criterion-based assessment
- ipsative assessment?

How to report:
- standard forms
- profiles
- free expression

How to use the information:
- to plan future work (formative assessment)
- as a summary of achievement (summative assessment)
- to identify problems (diagnostic assessment)?

Table 4.1: Developing a framework for assessment

they find they need to perform). These are called Reading, Writing, and Number Diets. These need not be kept continuously, but it is useful to ask for them at regular intervals, such as every three months for a few days or one week. They will provide a benchmark of learners' progress and a clue to the sort of reading, writing, and calculating that learners do, and need to do, to operate effectively outside the classroom.

It might help to remember the following points when deciding on a system for keeping records:

- Decide what suits you and the learners best.
- Keep it simple, so that it is not too time-consuming to be practical.

- Don't write more than is needed. It can be a short note to yourself or to the learners. As long as there is sufficient information to help you recall the points, it will do.
- Records can be tape-recorded or consist of a photocopy of learners' work.
- The records are reminders for you and the learners. They do not need to be immaculate.
- Encourage discussion.
- Involve the learners as much as possible. Act as a scribe if needed, but encourage them to keep their own records.
- Make it part of learning.
- Keep a note of unusual events or 'critical incidents', such as an individual breakthrough or a good idea that occurred to you.

By spending a little time on planning for assessment and evaluation at this early stage, you will enable yourself and the learners to keep track of what is happening, in practical ways that will help you throughout the programme.

PART THREE

Exploring Teaching and Learning

An evening class for resettled refugees in El Salvador
Photo: Jenny Matthews

CHAPTER 5

Some methods for teaching literacy

Working with adults

This book is concerned with the teaching of adults. Much research has been done on how adults learn and on appropriate ways of working with them. In some respects, methods of teaching adults differ from ways of working with children. What do we now know about how adults learn?

Some facts about adults' learning styles

* Adults are thought to learn more quickly than children; they already have a system for 'making sense' of things, and fitting their learning into what they already know.

* Children in most areas of the world see 'experience' as something that happens to them; they expect to be told what to do. Adults, in most cases, need to play a part in shaping their own experience; they prefer not to be told what to do.

* Children generally depend on someone else for their safety and livelihood. Adults generally have learnt to fend for themselves.

* Children have a limited experience of life. Much that they come across is new or strange to them. Adults have had a lifetime's experience of dealing with the new and the strange; they have already developed strategies for dealing with such things. But these strategies can also slow down the process of learning: adults may have developed set ideas about things, which will take time to change. They may need to unlearn habits built up over a lifetime, in order to adapt to new situations.

* In teaching children new things, it is helpful to base lessons on things they already know. Similarly, in helping adults to learn new things, their existing experience should not be ignored.

* Adults learn more successfully when the learning is relevant to their lives: when they can see the need for it and recognise how they will use it.

When working with adults, try to focus on learning rather than teaching. A literacy programme should be concerned with setting up a situation in which adults can learn.

Three ways in which adults learn

Adults who have not been to school will have learnt life skills in a variety of ways: by *listening and then doing*; by *trying for themselves* — by discovering how to do something; by *watching and imitating*. Different individuals learn best in different ways, and most people will have a preference for one of these three learning styles. Teachers can help to cater for individual preferences by varying the approaches to learning used on a literacy programme.

All three approaches to learning are useful learning strategies, but they should all be accompanied by discussion. Adults need to understand *why* they are doing something, and how it will be useful. They need to be given some responsibility for the learning process if they are to become confident and independent learners.

Discussing and challenging new information are important activities in the process of building confidence and independence. A good literacy worker will encourage a group to question rather than accept what they are told, and to judge its relevance in terms of their own experience. Handling a discussion is not easy; some skill is required on the part of the leader:

- to allow the group to take over the direction of the class;
- to stand back while people talk;
- to encourage everyone to say something;
- to stop any one person from dominating the group;
- to summarise the main points of what has been said;
- to get the group back together and move on.

Cultural constraints on adults' learning

People's expectations of learning and teaching are culturally determined, and affected by their previous experience. For example, some Koranic schools use repetition and rote learning as a way of memorising information. Children in such a school will be taught to repeat lines of the Koran aloud. This habit of chanting and repeating has its place, but is often transferred into literacy classes, where students may be asked to say a letter over and over again. As a method, it has little value when learning to read or to write.

Most formal schooling requires children to sit in rows at desks in front of the teacher, although chairs and tables may not be common in the households in the area. Students in a literacy class may be more comfortable sitting on the ground, as they would do if reading or writing at home; others may expect to use desks, if they use similar tables and chairs at home. Whatever the initial expectations of students, experience

Rows of desks are not usually the best arrangement for adult learners. Many will feel more comfortable sitting on the ground or — as here, in Tigray, Ethiopia — sitting round a table.
Photo: Neil Cooper

shows that rows of desks are not the best arrangement for adults. A suggested seating arrangement is given in Chapter 4.

Formal education in schools generally presents teachers as more powerful and more important than students. Students are in most cases required to accept rather than to question the information they are given. Anything written in a book may be seen as 'true', and students may be reluctant to challenge this assumption.

Adults who have had previous experience of organised learning (for example if they have completed one or two years of primary school, or if their children have attended school) may find the teaching methods used in a literacy class very different. The literacy worker may need to challenge their expectations and encourage them to think about how they actually learn, as distinct from how they expect to be taught.

Why do these learners need literacy?

The learning activities that take place in a literacy class will be determined partly by the purposes for which literacy will be used. As far as possible, learning activities should be based on the practice of literacy in real situations, using real examples.

For instance, students who need to learn how to keep accounts should be introduced to them as soon as possible. Activities can be based on filling in a range of real or invented details on account sheets. It is easier see the relevance of learning numbers when they are placed in the context of the learners' lives.

Students who want to learn to write letters should try writing them as soon as possible. They can begin with activities which involve them in dictating and copying, adding characters they know, and looking over their own letters written for them by someone else. A 'real' activity, or a simulated activity that has a real aim, is almost always better than an invented exercise. Remember that adults learn best by doing something, rather than just hearing about doing it.

What kind of literacy do they need?

The various types of learning that take place in a literacy class will include skills of reading, writing, and calculating. Students will be presented with themes or information about certain topics, such as information about bee-keeping, or book-keeping, or using a public library. They will acquire self-confidence in using literacy activities in everyday life, for instance when using a post office or a bank.

The various skills and the themes chosen by the group will probably be taught alongside each other. But, whatever skills and themes are developed within a class or learning programme, they should be closely related to the use of those techniques and topics in a real-life situation. Skills are not automatically transferable. Literacy workers, concentrating on teaching the material they have prepared, too often forget to relate that material to what people see in the village, or in their homes.

Between classes or meetings, learners should be encouraged to look for street notices, signboards, political posters, sweet wrappings, etc. The worker should begin with the expectation that the group will use their literacy skills outside the classroom. They may begin their programme by learning letters or words, but they can still be encouraged, from the first session, to try to identify a similar letter or word, in a different type-face or size, somewhere outside the class.

Most important of all, students should be encouraged from the beginning to question and debate what they read, and to analyse, question, and cross-check the results of their number work. For some students, a literacy class may be an end in itself. For others it will be the first step in a continuing learning programme. In either case, it is important to avoid dependency on the literacy worker. As far as possible, students should be encouraged to think and to decide for themselves, and to set their own standards. The aim of a good tutor is to become dispensable!

What methods should the programme use?

There is no one 'correct' method. Every time a method is chosen, it carries with it a number of assumptions. Any choice of method will depend on how planners and tutors perceive students, how they conceive of knowledge, and how far they want to retain or share power.

A large number of literacy programmes throughout the world are based on a primer — that is, a book planned and printed in advance of the local programme, containing a new lesson on every page. Students generally work through it from beginning to end.

Using a primer has several advantages.

- Students can see their progress.
- It makes things easier for tutors, who can base their sessions on the structure of the book.
- Literacy workers who may have had little training in teaching can be shown how to work to a set formula.

On the other hand, using a primer has its disadvantages.

- It will have been planned by trainers, rather than by the users of a programme.
- It may have little relevance to what students in the group want or feel they need to learn.
- The focus is on progressing through the book, rather than on guiding the group to learn things that they can use.
- Information comes to be seen as something fixed and pre-determined, rather than something that students discover for themselves.

Methods for teaching literacy will be discussed in full below. Planners and tutors will be encouraged to work without a primer, or, where a primer is already available, to use it selectively, questioning with students the value of its contents.

Approaches to literacy

Any decision about which learning method or methods to use in a literacy programme will need to take into account the structure of the language, and how writing relates to speech. Many early languages used images or small pictures, like Egyptian hieroglyphics, which gave a visual indication of the object being referred to. The classical Chinese script is derived from such an ideographic system of writing, and contains many pictorial elements. However, modern Chinese characters now relate partly to sounds and not entirely to concepts or things. Individual Chinese characters represent parts of words as well as whole words, and a teaching approach that focused on individual words, rather than meaning, could not be sustained. Basic literacy in present-day Chinese entails learning about 2,000 individual characters.

Alphabetic writing systems, such as Arabic, Roman, and Hindi scripts, use symbols or letters to determine a spoken sound. Most alphabets contain between 20 and 30 symbols; the exact numbers vary according to the degree of complexity in the sound system of the language in question. Some languages have a direct relationship between the letter and the sound representing it: Spanish, for example, is a strongly phonetic language, while English is not. Languages which were traditionally oral and have been written down only recently — such as Pulaar, Kiswahili, and Wolof — use a writing system that is almost directly representative. Unlike, say, French, these languages have not been subject to complex changes of pronunciation over a long period of time; unlike, say, English, they have not been exposed to long periods of contact with other written languages. English, because of its complex history, has a very indirect relationship between letter and sound. Becoming literate in English presents problems with spelling that are not experienced in more directly phonetic languages.

Some alphabetic languages, like Hebrew and Arabic, represent only the consonant sounds in writing: the marking of vowels is optional. Others, such as Hindi, do indicate vowel sounds — but only as small marks, not as separate letters.

Literacy programmes in alphabetic languages need to take into account several crucial factors:

- *The relationship between the name of the letter and its sound.* In English, the name of the letter A is different from the way in which it sounds in some words: consider, for example, the sounds in *apple, arm,* and *bead.* In cases like this, students can become confused if required to learn the alphabet (the names of the letters) first.

- *Whether letters change when used in combination with other letters.* For example, *g*, when used before *h*, as in *high*, represents hardly any sound at all.

- *The relationship between individual words and meanings.* Most languages add endings (suffixes) or beginnings (prefixes) to words, to indicate such things as plurality, tense, and size.

- *The ease with which words break down into individual syllables.* English, for example, does not always differentiate clearly between syllables, largely because some syllables in multi-syllabic words carry a very weak stress. Spanish, and other more regularly phonetic languages, tend to have a much more regular stress pattern. For example:

  English: *el-e-ment* (the middle syllable is barely sounded)
  Spanish: *el-e-ment-o* (all syllables carry equal weight).

- *Where a word begins and ends.* Many languages, particularly the Germanic ones, form compound words by joining together two or more individual words. A good example of this is the German expression *fußballweltmeisterschaftsmannschaftsauswahl*, which means 'football world championship team selection'. A teaching method which begins with the learning of individual words will need to make this tendency explicit.

- *The use of capital letters.* The Roman alphabet uses capital letters which, in many cases, look different from the small letters which they relate to: *a A, b B, d D,* etc. A letter-based approach to literacy should consider which letter-forms to start with, or whether to teach both alongside each other.

Reading, writing, and calculating

Reading, writing, and calculating involve different skills. The skills involved in reading are mainly those of recognising, decoding, and understanding what has been written by someone else. They also involve reacting to the information that has been read, and making use of it. This is generally the case, regardless of which writing system is being used.

The skills involved in writing are more demanding: most people learn to read sooner and more easily than they learn to write. Learning to write involves mastering manual manipulation of a pen or pencil; remembering the exact form of a letter or character and recreating it; and transferring thoughts into signs, in order to write something down.

The skills involved in numeracy are different again. Although they include recognising and reproducing signs and symbols, the symbols represent quantity and have no relationship to their spoken form. In this sense they are like Chinese characters. Being numerate means not only recognising and recording numbers, but manipulating them to create other numbers that represent other amounts, i.e. 'doing sums'. Many adults can do mental arithmetic, even though they may not be able to write numbers down. Before deciding what to teach, it is important to discover what learners already know and how they currently deal with number concepts.

Generally, but not necessarily, adults use skills of reading, writing, and calculating in combination with each other. The combination of skills needed by the learners will help to determine which methods should be used to acquire which skills, and in what order. Most programmes work with a combination of methods.

Whichever methods are used, it is important to start with what students already know. All students will know something of either reading, writing, counting, or encoding. They will all have some idea of the uses and value of recording, of who does it, where, and why. They will all be able to recognise some form of sign. In an urban society, where written communication is part of the environment, students will be familiar with many images, words, letters, or signs, even though they may not know what they stand for. (The signs for Coca Cola, Toyota, and Singer are almost universal.)

Billboards in Santo Domingo: in an urban society, written communication is part of the environment.
Photo: Richard English

Taking time to find out what students already know, feel, think, recognise, and understand is the best way to start. Any future learning, using any method, can begin here.

Try to analyse how different skills are used in different circumstances. Reading a telephone directory is not the same as reading a newspaper, and a different skill again is required in reading a personal letter. Writing a letter or recording personal thoughts or events are different from copying something or filling in a form. Writing down numbers or recording amounts is a far simpler process than adding, subtracting, or dividing large quantities, working out percentages, or calculating areas.

But becoming literate involves more than learning a set of skills. Understanding how and when those skills are used, and by whom, what is done with them, and the conclusions that can be drawn from them is part of a continuous learning process.

Being literate is not just knowing how to read and write and calculate, but knowing how to incorporate these skills into the common practice of everyday life. For people who have grown up in a family or an environment where this has not been the case, taking on literacy practices is a much bigger task.

Approaches to teaching reading and writing

Approaches to teaching reading and writing can be divided into two broad categories:

- **'bottom-up' approaches**: those that start with learning a single unit, such as a letter, character, or syllable, which is later combined with others, to build up words or sentences; the main focus is on recognising and 'decoding' elements of text;

- **'top-down' approaches**: those that start with learning a unit of meaning, such as a word or a sentence, which is later broken down into individual letters or characters; the main focus is on meaning.

These two approaches are illlustrated in Figure 5.1. People who support a 'bottom-up' approach to learning claim that learners need to be familiar with the elements of reading and writing (individual letters and characters) before they start to write or read text that is meaningful. It is not unusual for learners to start with pen-strokes (for example, horizontal and vertical strokes for languages using a Roman alphabet, joined-up strokes moving from right to left for those using Arabic script), before learning how they form letters. While this approach may mean that it is easier to master individual letters initially, it has been criticised for slowing readers down in the long term. People who have been taught to pay attention to individual letters and sound out each one may always see letters individually, and never become fast and fluent readers.

People who support a 'top-down' approach to literacy stress that it is easier to recognise or remember things that have meaning. Fluent

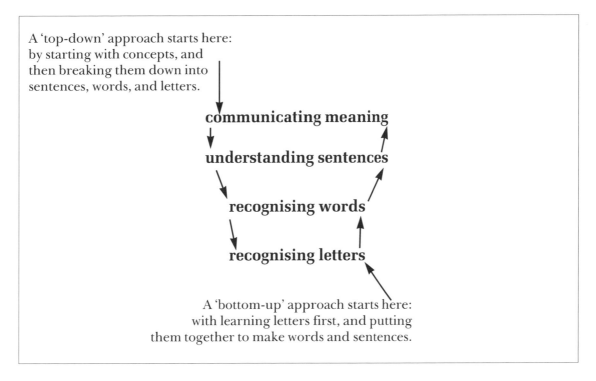

A 'top-down' approach starts here: by starting with concepts, and then breaking them down into sentences, words, and letters.

communicating meaning

understanding sentences

recognising words

recognising letters

A 'bottom-up' approach starts here: with learning letters first, and putting them together to make words and sentences.

readers and writers do not focus on individual letters, and do not remember individual pen strokes. Readers recognise words and groups of words, and are more likely to remember and understand those that are grouped in a way that actually says and means something, i.e. those that are arranged into a sentence, and those that deal with information which the learners are concerned about.

In practice, most people approaching literacy for the first time will use a combination of methods, moving between them to find what works best for them at different times. But regardless of the structure of the language, the alternatives presented in Figure 5.1 can be a useful starting point for considering the best approach. It helps to ascertain whether learners would find it easier to start with the smallest unit in a language and build up from there, or to start with letters or characters that carry a specific meaning and communicate something to the reader.

Figure 5.1:
Two approaches to
reading and writing[14]

'Bottom-up' approaches

Learning letters

Literacy programmes that start with the teaching of letters form part of the 'bottom-up' approach. Classes in languages such as Chinese or Nepali would begin with the strokes that make up a character. Classes in languages like English, which use an alphabet, can begin with the *names* of letters (the alphabetic approach) or the *sounds* of the letters (the phonic approach). As the name and the sound are rarely the same, the value in stressing the names of letters has been questioned.

apple : /a/

apple

Figure 5.2

It may not be uncommon to hear groups chanting the alphabet, and some learners may expect to have to do this. But merely knowing the alphabet is of little practical use. As an arrangement of letters, it bears no relationship to either their sounds or the frequency with which they are used. Workers who use it in their classes may be imitating the way in which they themselves were taught at school. A better approach to teaching letters is generally to begin with letter *sounds*.

A VSO volunteer in Nepal writes:

The alphabetic method for teaching reading is common in Nepali schools. Children learning to read in English first learn the names of the 26 letters. They then learn to read and spell a word by naming and memorising the letters which compose it. The phonic method has become more acceptable elsewhere ... In trying to understand why Nepali teachers are so hooked on the alphabetic method, (we) questioned (them) ... they said they themselves were confused about the phonics and felt unconfident about using letter sounds, so they felt happier using the letter names and chanting.

Learning sounds

The phonic approach is still one of the most commonly used methods throughout the world. It generally begins by presenting the shape of a letter, and indicating the sound it makes. Sometimes picture alphabets are used as reminders. These present either a letter alongside a picture of something beginning with that letter (Figure 5.2), or a letter form written on top of something that shares its shape (as in figure 5.3). The purpose of combining letters and objects in this way is to attach a meaning to a letter shape and therefore make it easier to remember. While this sometimes happens, the effort to find a meaningful shape for every letter may mean that the links are very artificial. A literacy worker, trying to teach the meaning of the image and the way in which it relates to the letter, as well as the letter itself, is likely to leave learners feeling very confused. If the link is not obvious as an aid to memory, it might be better to avoid stressing it. Primers using this method should be used selectively.

Another danger in this method is that, when learning different letters in pairs, learners will continue to associate them together and will confuse them with each other.

Another method is to group letters according to their sound and their function on a letter chart. This can be done only with a phonetic

Figure 5.3:
Part of a picture
alphabet

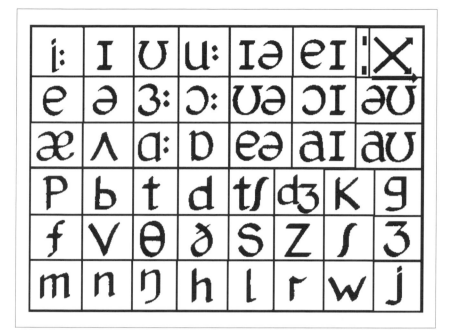

*Figure 5.4:
International
Phonetic Alphabet,
arranged according to
letter sounds and letter
functions[15]*

language, i.e. one in which a single letter represents a single sound. Figure 5.4 uses the international phonetic alphabet. Here the letters have been arranged according to the sounds they represent. The lower half of the chart represents consonant sounds. These have been paired, with similar sounds (such as /p/ and /b/, which are called 'unvoiced' and 'voiced') arranged next to each other.

The symbols on the top left-hand side of the chart represent vowel sounds. These have also been paired, with long and short vowel sounds (i and i:) arranged next to each other. The symbols on the top right-hand side of the chart represent diphthongs, or 'double vowel' sounds. The symbols in the far right-hand square are used to represent stress and intonation. This chart was devised for teaching English to non-native speakers, and is used mainly to correct pronunciation, where stress and intonation are very important.

*Figure 5.5:
A letter chart for the
Pulaar alphabet*

The chart in Figure 5.5, showing the Pulaar alphabet, has been arranged differently, and is based on columns. The first two columns contain pairs of letters (unvoiced and voiced), and indicate consonant sounds. The third, single column contains the 'hooked' letters (pronounced at the back of the throat). The fourth, single column contains the double consonant sounds. The last, paired columns contain letters which represent long and short vowel sounds.

P	b	c	j	ɓ	nd	i	ii
t	d	r	y	ɗ	mb	u	uu
k	g	m	n	ƴ	nj	a	aa
f	w	s		ŋ	ŋg	o	oo
h	l	' / .	?	q	ñ	e	ee

63

The lowest squares of the second column are used for a full stop, a comma, and a question mark. As this chart was devised for teaching writing to native speakers, these were added to show some of the most commonly used punctuation marks. A similar chart could be created, showing capital letters, to enable learners to indicate when and where they might use them; or the blank square could be used to denote 'capitalisation'.

The exact organisation of letters in a chart will vary according to the sounds they represent, and the relationship between sound, letter, and meaning in the language as a whole.

A chart such as Figure 5.5, displayed in a learning room, can serve as a continual reminder of the sounds and shapes of letters. It can be used when presenting new letters or correcting a learner's work. By pointing to the characters on the chart, learners can be encouraged to sound out and spell out new words.

Some programmes begin by teaching vowels (a, e, i, o, u, in a Roman alphabet) and then move on to consonants (b, c, d, f, g, h, j, k, l, m, n, p, q, r, s, t, v, w, x, y, z). These are then put together in pairs to make sounds, which students are often asked to repeat: ba/be/bi/bo/bu. While this exercise shows how individual letter sounds can be combined to make new sounds, the endless repetition of meaningless sounds is of little value. Many literacy groups spend time chanting together such sequences as

ba/ba/ba/
be/be/be/
bo/bo/bo/ ...

but it is questionable whether anything useful is being learned. In English, where the written language is not phonetic and /bo/ can represent a long sound as in *boot*, a short sound as in *book*, or an open sound as in *boat*, this exercise is worse than useless. In a language such as this, an approach that begins with learning sentences or words may be more effective.

In learning to write letters first, learners need to appreciate the *process* of writing as well as the end product. In writing with a pen or a pencil, letters will eventually be written in groups, and each language has its own common combination of groups. Writing fluently involves joining letters up, and therefore making the individual strokes of a letter in a certain order. Letters are sometimes taught with this in mind, by indicating the direction of pen strokes. (See Figure 5.6.)

Learners will also eventually need to recognise a series of different letter forms (within the Roman alphabet this includes capital and lower-case letters, A and a) and the different appearance of letters in different type faces: a and a. Most writing and reading tasks involve both capital and lower-case letters. It may be easier to introduce capital and lower-case letters at the same time, and not as two separate alphabets.

Although all learners will need to learn individual letters or characters eventually, a programme that begins by teaching letters may take some time to introduce real words or sentences. It can be hard for learners to stay motivated, unless learning is linked in some way to reality.

*Figure 5.6:
A page from a primer
used in Tamil Nadu,
India*

One main reason for using a letter-based approach is its tight and logical structure. Literacy workers can be trained to use it in a relatively short time, and it does not involve a lot of creativity or pre-planned work.

Learning syllables

It is less common for tutors to begin with teaching syllables, though this can work well with languages that have a very definite phonetic and/or syllabic structure, i.e. languages that are written exactly as they sound. Teaching syllables means breaking down languages into the smallest element that can be heard; for example

ra/re/ri/ro/ru.

Once learners become familiar with a number of syllables, they can put them together and use them to create words; for example

re + lay = relay.

This method cannot be used effectively with English, or with languages like Chinese where characters represent the meaning rather than the sound of a word. It can work with traditionally oral languages that have been written down with an orthography which matches the sound. It can also be used with some long-established phonetic languages, such as Spanish, where the spelling of a word is accurately based on its sound:

ten-go que a-pren-der a es-cri-bir.

However, there is a danger that people learning in this way will get stuck in the habit of sounding out every syllable as they read, and not see words and sentences as whole units. This method sets up an association

65

between writing and speech (i.e. sound), rather than between writing and meaning.

As a relatively simple, tightly structured approach, teaching syllables is generally more popular with tutors and literacy workers than with learners. It is often used in connection with other methods, particularly with the teaching of key words (see below).

'Top-down' approaches

Learning words

An approach that begins with individual words can focus either on 'decoding' (or recognising) written word patterns, or on reading for meaning. The first is closer to the 'bottom-up' way of looking at language. The second tends to see words as the smallest meaningful unit in written language, and then works downwards. Both can be used with ideographic and phonetic languages.

As a method, learning whole words is often part of a highly controlled approach to literacy, and generally begins with reading rather than writing. In almost every language, about 80 per cent of almost everything that is written consists of a vocabulary of around 100 to 150 words. Some reading schemes introduce students to these most common words first. The schemes are based on the belief that new readers will feel more confident when they can understand a large proportion of a written text. But learners who are taught to approach text in this way are still generally 'decoding' what they see in front of them, and not reading for meaning. The common words in a language (words like *a, and, but, the, if, not,* etc. in English) carry very little meaning in isolation. It is the new or individual words (such as nouns and verbs) that give the most useful clues to what the text is about. Learners who begin with 'common word' patterns will not easily develop strategies to decipher the new words.

Some schemes are based on a set vocabulary, which is introduced at predetermined intervals: for example, five words in the first lesson, and 15 per lesson after that. They may use a lot of repetition to reinforce the new words, and 'look and say' activities such as seeing and naming words. Words are often written out on individual cards (called 'flash cards' in English), to be flashed in front of learners in an attempt to establish familiar visual patterns which they will then remember. It is a highly structured approach, emphasising repetition and familiarity, rather than treating written language as something which is meaningful.

An alternative to this is the 'key word' approach. It still begins with individual words, but it uses words that have a particular significance for the people learning them, rather than words that are common or easy to learn. Research has shown that adults and children can and do learn to recognise long and complex words without difficulty, if they want or need to read or write them.

The Brazilian educator, Paulo Freire, developed the use of what he called 'generative words' for literacy learning. These were words which he felt had a particular cultural or social significance for the group, such

*Paulo Freire
(second from right) at
a literacy workshop in
Brazil.*
Photo: Oxfam

as 'poverty', 'homelessness', or 'fear'. The words were used as a springboard for discussion at the beginning of each teaching session, and often in connection with an image depicting an aspect of the learners' life.

A picture is shown to the group, who are encouraged to discuss it and to question the concepts which are 'codified' or embedded within it. Sometimes the key word is presented to the group by the teacher; sometimes it arises out of the group's discussion of the picture. But the word is eventually written up, repeated, and broken down into syllables and then letters. The syllables can be used to create other words, in which learners might be encouraged to identify individual letters — and the letters are used to write new words.

Freire stressed that reading is more than understanding written language. It entails gaining an understanding of the social, economic, and political situation in which the learners find themselves, and the causes behind that situation. By using 'generative words', he encouraged his groups to question not only written information, but the potential for change within their lives. By starting with words that were emotive and meaningful, he aimed to ensure that reading and writing could be more closely associated with central issues in people's lives.

Sylvia Ashton-Warner, who taught Maori children in New Zealand, used a different word-based approach to literacy. She asked individual children to choose the words they wanted to learn. Each chosen word was then written on a card and given to the child to 'keep'. If the child misbehaved, the words were taken away as a punishment, and later returned as rewards. Each child built up a store of his or her own words which, because they were personally meaningful, were seldom forgotten. They were used as a basis for creative writing, where the children were encouraged to develop their thoughts and ideas around the words they had chosen. The '100 most common words' in a language were therefore taught incidentally, as children put their 'significant words' into sentences.

Learning sentences

An approach that starts with learning sentences is often known as a 'global method'. It is based on the idea that a sentence is the smallest 'whole thought', and therefore the most meaningful and easiest to remember. While this may be true, and the approach aims to work with 'meaningful material', learners may still find themselves memorising and repeating sentences, rather than actually reading them, for quite a long time.

Tutors working in a less structured way often begin with a picture or image, as in the 'key word' approach. The discussion of this image may take up a large part of the learning session. From this the group formulates its own key sentence, to sum up what has been said. Where this method is based on the work of Freire, which was originally designed for use in Portuguese — a syllabic language — the key sentence is then often broken down into words, syllables, and eventually letters. In this way, students are introduced to the different units which make up written language.

It is more common to find this method used with images and key sentences prepared in advance and published as a primer, with a number of learning exercises. The images can still be used in discussion in a

Figure 5.7:
'Before selling grain,
keep back enough for
seed and for food': a
page from a Pulaar
primer, showing a key
sentence, a key word,
a key syllable, and
today's key letter

ko adii nde njeeyataa joñ aawdi e ŋguura.
njeeyataa
njee ya taa
njee
nj

similar way, but the key sentence may have been designed to introduce specific new letters, and the various exercises already worked out. The sentences therefore give a predetermined interpretation of the image. (See Figure 5.7.)

As a teaching method, the 'key sentence' approach has been widely and successfully used. Tutors working with it are generally taught to plan each lesson round a set image, a sentence, and a subsequent exercise. It is relatively easy to introduce to new tutors with the minimum amount of training. Literacy workers are able to lead their groups through the primer, and need few other materials. However, such pre-structured sessions do less to encourage independence or involvement on the part of the learners, and do not leave space for them to consider what they want to learn. Instead, this approach prepackages the views of the planners about what and how much can be covered in one time.

The REFLECT methodology

In 1993, ACTIONAID began an action research project to explore the possible uses of participatory rural appraisal (PRA) within adult literacy programmes. This has led to the development of the REFLECT methodology: Regenerated Freirean Literacy through Empowering Community Techniques. REFLECT seeks to build on Freirean theory, but provides a structured methodology to help learners to achieve their goals.

In a REFLECT programme there are no primers, and no pre-printed materials, apart from the facilitator's guide. Each literacy class develops its own learning materials, by constructing maps, matrices, calendars, and diagrams, representing different aspects of community experience. In Uganda, for example, these range from a gender-workload calendar to a crop-ranking matrix, constructed on the ground by the whole group, using local materials (sticks, flowers, stones, etc.).

This process pools and organises learners' existing knowledge, promoting detailed analysis of local issues. It helps the literacy worker to structure the dialogue, by handing over the process to the participants, and not being forced to lead the group to a prescribed conclusion. It is, in addition, an enjoyable activity for adult learners.

After the calendar or diagram has been constructed, the literacy worker replaces the sticks and stones with visual cards; this is the first stage of literacy. The diagram is then transferred to a large piece of paper, using the visual symbols already agreed by the class. At this stage the literacy and numeracy activities formally begin.

Learners label and number the diagram, use words and phrases from their discussion for practice in reading and writing, and are soon able to write independently, experimenting with various combinations of the syllables and words covered. The course is planned so that basic syllables (in the language chosen by the learners for literacy) can be taught in a logical order, but everything comes from the vocabulary universe of the learners themselves. People who advocate the method claim that the vocabulary is easy to retain, because it occurs in a meaningful context.

A work-load exercise in Uganda: participatory rural appraisal in action.
Photo: Sam Gonda

Supplementary 'real' reading materials are also introduced on the themes covered in the discussions, so that learners can practise at home. In Uganda, low-cost printing of learner-generated materials has already begun, and this is seen as a major contribution to sustaining literacy. In addition, every literacy class and every individual has a detailed record of their discussions, in both visual and written forms.

The REFLECT project has been run initially as a two-year pilot in very different contexts. In Uganda, it is operating in a multilingual area where neither of the two main local languages was previously written down. In Bangladesh, it is being used in women's savings and credit groups in a conservative Islamic area. In El Salvador it has been piloted with a grassroots NGO led by former guerrillas.

Learning what you need (the Language Experience Approach)

Another way of working from the language of learners, which has been used over a longer period of time in industrialised countries, is the 'Language Experience Approach'. In this system, a learner says what she or he wants to see written down. It might be a short phrase, a sentence, or even several sentences. The learner often goes on to dictate it, while the tutor copies it, and then uses the text as the basis for a variety of learning exercises. The learner can be encouraged to 'read' individual words in sequence. The words can then be cut up and identified separately. Words can be copied, analysed into letters or sounds, or used in other combinations to make different sentences.

The Language Experience Approach can be used with two people working together, or by a literacy worker with a group (in which case, individuals take turns to dictate the material that will form the basis of the learning).

This approach has considerable advantages. It gives the learners some power: from the beginning they are the 'creators' as well as the 'decoders' of the written word. It takes some of the mystique out of writing. It makes strong connections between written and spoken language. But this approach presents its own difficulties. Working with language generated by the students requires a lot more skill and creativity on the part of the tutor. Literacy workers cannot prepare their lessons in advance in the same way as they can when using a primer. They need to be creative and inventive in order to turn any fragments of language into learning exercises, and to break them down and build them up in a way that the class can manage.

In most languages, the way people write is different from the way people speak. Taking a Language Experience approach means that literacy workers have to be aware of, and ready to explain, these differences. They need the confidence to abandon any formal approaches to teaching which they may have remembered from school, and to work with what the learners need.

In the same way, learners need more confidence in themselves, and their own ability to tackle the literacy tasks relevant to their needs. Without a primer to read between classes, they have to be encouraged to practise their literacy on the written words, signs, notices, and leaflets which they find around them. They will have to bring in with them material which they can recognise, or want to read, rather than take out with them material that development workers feel they ought to read.

Using the Language Experience Approach is certainly a risk. It puts fewer demands on material resources, and higher demands on human resources. Literacy workers will need longer and more thorough training courses. They will need the time and support to experiment, and the opportunity to be creative.

But while the risks are higher, the rewards are also higher. Learners are involved in creating materials from the beginning. Some of this can be copied and used by others (see the section on learner-generated materials in Chapter 10). The learning of literacy is linked, from the beginning, to the practice of literacy in real situations in people's lives. The repetition and rote learning that often accompanies primers is replaced by breaking down and building up the things that people really need to write or read.

Conclusion

This chapter has presented an outline of some of the methods used for teaching literacy. It will be clear that the writers of this book tend to favour those methods where students are given as much choice as possible in determining what and how they will learn. In this way, their motivation is likely to be greater than cases where they simply follow what they are told to do, or where they repeat letters, sounds, or syllables by rote. However, given the great complexity of the world's languages and cultures, any choice must take the local language and cultural practices into account. Without this, it is not possible to make a choice at all. Even then, the choice of literacy method is often controversial, and it may be best to experiment with a combination of methods according to circumstances.

CHAPTER 6

Learning numbers and reading images

Traditional and indigenous concepts of number

Approaches to teaching numeracy are usually based on the traditional conception of maths in the Western world. They generally start by representing quantity:

Figure 6.1

and move on to addition and subtraction:

1 banana + 2 bananas = 3 bananas

These are presented as traditional 'sums':

1 + 2 = 3

or as problem-solving activities:

You are given four bananas; your brother eats one; how many have you got left?

Approaches of this kind start by assuming either that learners know nothing, or that what they know is based on a Western conception of number. The truth is, of course, that systems of 'indigenous mathematics' have served people well for thousands of years in their daily lives: every culture has evolved ways of dealing with quantitative problems, such as calculating time, distance, weight, number, and value.

A recognition that people everywhere have to deal with quantitative problems in some way provides a different starting point to the teaching of formal numeracy.

When starting to plan a survey to assess numeracy needs, it will be useful to look at any research that might have been done into local methods of calculating. This can be explored further by taking a problem-solving approach.

> L.S. Saraswathi did some research in India, investigating how adults without literacy skills solved daily quantitative problems. She looked at riddles, stories, songs, and games for evidence of localised modes of learning. Children's rhymes, clapping games, or jumping games often show how they learn to mark time or deal with turn-taking. Riddles give some insight into local approaches to problem-solving. Saraswathi asked how people perceive time, and how they measure time. She began by asking which of a series of events takes most time (to drink a glass of water, to pass something to someone in front of you, to walk to the next village) and how people described the amount of time which each event took. She asked people when they were born, when their children were born, and how they determined age. She looked at how people recorded events in the past, how they kept records of money and accounts, and how they calculated profit and loss in the market place.

A children's counting game in Mozambique. Every culture has evolved ways of dealing with the quantitative problems of daily life.
Photo: Susie Smith

Problem-solving approaches to teaching numeracy

A good way to access local knowledge is to begin a class with an everyday problem and ask the group to solve it.

- How do you decide on the amount of seed needed to sow a field?
- If you had to sow your brother's field also, how much seed would you need?
- If you had to sow the fields of everyone in this room, how much seed would you need?

The group may want to work with an abacus, or beads, shells, or stones to show how they would deal with their problem. Numeracy and number work are about relationship and representation, the representation of a quantity with a figure, and the relationship of one number to another. Each culture will have its own way of representing quantity. Many will have developed their own system of representation, by cutting notches in wood or collecting beads in jars. Learners will be familiar with the convention of representing one thing with another. They can be encouraged to discuss their indigenous codes and compare them with numerical representation.

Beginning with problems provides some insight into what knowledge local people already have, and what knowledge they might want. Encouraging learners to solve problems aloud, by talking through the various steps used in solving a numerical problem, reveals the strategies they currently use, and where they might be going wrong.

Learners should be encouraged to work with real problems, or those that simulate real situations. It is generally preferable to use examples which learners themselves have suggested, or situations they will actually need to deal with in their lives. It may be difficult for them to see the point in tackling unfamiliar problems, such as the following:

> *I buy a jacket costing £25.00. If I find a similar one in another shop that is £5.00 cheaper, how much does the second jacket cost?*

Though questions like these may be familiar to people who have been through formal schooling, they are of little value in rural contexts. Even if learners are in a position to buy an expensive jacket and deal with fixed-price goods, it is unlikely that they will need to work out this problem in this way.

Estimating

Adults without formal numeracy skills may be used to calculating by instinct, touch, or feel. They may know the amount of water and time needed to irrigate a field, or when meat is cooked, without being able to attach a numerical quantity to it. Estimating is an important skill in itself, when checking whether or not the answer to a mathematical sum is correct. It is useful to make a connection between the informal estimations which people make naturally, by eye, and the more formal processes of measuring amount, quantity, size, time, or value.

For example, when introducing concepts of distance, ask learners to estimate how far it is in yards/miles/metres/kilometres between where they are sitting and the chalk board, between their house and the literacy building, between the literacy building and the hospital, between the village and the capital, between one country and another.

When introducing formal concepts of capacity, show the learners a number of containers. Ask them to lay these out in order of size, from the smallest to the largest. Ask them to estimate the capacity (in pints, millilitres, or litres) of each container.

Giving the learners actual examples helps to make use of their natural ability to estimate, while at the same time making the concept of numbers real.

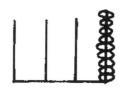

Figure 6.2:
An abacus. If space is allowed for only nine beads or stones in each section, it can be demonstrated that ten can be represented by just one bead in the next section.

Number functions

Recognising numbers

After the literacy worker has identified a real problem that learners need to solve, the task should be broken down into the various skills or actual number tasks that are involved. One of the first of these is recognising, understanding, and writing the number shapes themselves.

Common problems

Initially learners may have problems with similar numbers, such as 6 and 9, 3 and 8 — especially if they have a tendency to write numbers back to front or upside down. In writing two-, three-, or four-digit numbers, learners need to understand the importance of number order; for example, 27 is different from 72.

Many learners have problems with the concept of nought or zero. The use of 0 in large numbers (730/2016/500, etc.) needs to be carefully explained and linked to real-life examples (such as the difference between 5, 50, and 500 people).

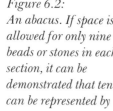

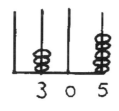

Figure 6.3:
An abacus is also useful for demonstrating the concept of 0 in large numbers.

In order to understand large numbers, learners need to be familiar with the number-base used. In the formal system of the majority of countries and cultures, the base is 10; but this may not be the case with indigenous counting. A simple abacus, either made of wood or marked out with stones on the sand, is useful in explaining this.

When dealing with time (seconds, minutes, hours, days, months, years), and with money in some cultures, units of ten no longer apply. For example:

20 hours + 35 hours + 7 hours = 62 hours (not 6 days and 2 hours)

25 days + 10 days + 23 hours + 5 hours + 1 day = 36 days and 28 hours = 37 days, 4 hours

Once learners are able to recognise and understand number concepts, they need to begin to manipulate the four basic number functions, addition, subtraction, multiplication, and division, and to appreciate the connections between them:

$4 + 3 = 7, 7 - 3 = 4$

$3 + 3 + 3 + 3 = 4 \times 3$

$4 \times 3 = 12, 12/3 = 4$

But these should be demonstrated by using examples and within the context of real problems.

- Can you estimate how much material you need to make a dress?
- Can you measure how much?
- How much does it cost per metre?
- How much will it cost for the number of metres you need?
- How much will it cost to make two dresses, one for your sister?
- Your sister is smaller, and will need one metre less material. How much money can you take off?
- Do you need to buy anything else, such as cotton or buttons? How much will it cost?
- Divide the cost equally between you and your sister.

It is important to work out problems in advance, before presenting them to learners, and to anticipate the obstacles they might encounter. These may be cultural as well as numerical; for example, is it acceptable to charge a sister for the materials for her dress? Do traders in the market-place measure in yards, metres, or arm's length?

Language

People who have been through formal schooling often adopt the special language used to describe number functions and the various steps involved in working out number problems. Some of the familiar phrases used in English schools include formulas like:

'Five into three won't go.'

'Put down the one and carry five.'

'Two plus seven makes nine.'

'Five times two is ten.'

This language can be confusing to learners who are unfamiliar with it. In itself it doesn't mean anything and needs to be explained. Similarly, when solving problems with learners, literacy workers need to take care to explain the steps they are working through. The unconscious use of mental arithmetic or multiplication tables can seem like magic and cause confusion when a learner is trying to get to grips with a problem.

Using calculators

Calculators are now in use almost everywhere in the world, and they are likely to form part of any numeracy programme. However, before being taught to use one, learners need to be familiar with what numbers are and what they can do. If learners are encouraged to use calculators in a merely mechanical way, they may fail to grasp the relationship between the numbers and the things which they represent.

Using a calculator does not remove the need for mental arithmetic.
Photo: Mike Goldwater

When using a calculator, learners need to understand several more or less sophisticated procedures:

- how to turn a calculator on and off;
- how to enter numbers (0-9, 10-100, etc.);
- how to enter sums of money, especially money not based on units of 10;
- how to cancel or change something that has been wrongly entered;
- how to add, subtract, multiply, and divide two numbers;
- how to add or multiply three or more numbers;
- the largest number that a calculator can show;
- what the numbers mean in real life.

Learners will also need to perform some mental arithmetic, in order to estimate whether the answer given by their calculator is a realistic one (since it is easy to tap in a wrong number or a wrong command). They need to know how to extract the actual number-functions from a problem, and how to convert numbers back into real concepts. For example:

A group of 75 people have decided to contribute towards a loan fund. They will make contributions every month, and every month one member can apply to use the money for something they need. If they contribute three shillings each a month, how much can each person borrow? If everyone needs to take turns to borrow money, how often can one person borrow?

75 x 3 = money available each month.

75/12 = years before one person is able to use the fund a second time.

Keeping accounts

Throughout history, literacy has been associated with trade and the need to keep records of produce sold. In many cultures, writing systems were developed initially as a system of accounting. In areas where co-operatives and credit groups are operating, members will need either to understand an existing system of book-keeping or to establish one for themselves.

Farmers involved in cultivating will need to keep records of:

- the supply of inputs
- the means of production
- costs involved in the management of water (fuel for a motor pump, a depreciation fund for a pump or sprinkler, etc.)
- weight of produce stored
- weight of produce sold
- value of produce stored and sold.

Savers involved in a credit group will need to keep records of:

- subscriptions from members
- interest paid on subscriptions (if any)
- withdrawals made by members
- the balance of the fund.

Any co-operative or group will have a treasurer responsible for the keeping of accounts, but in an equitable system all members will want to understand what is being done with their money.

Learners new to accounting need to understand the function of accounts, as well as learning how to keep them. Using them effectively entails dealing with addition, subtraction, multiplication, division, and decimals; it can involve quantities of time, weight, money, liquid measure, size, distance — in fact, most quantitative measures and most number functions. It means understanding the significance of recording information vertically, in columns, instead of horizontally, and learning the language and concepts of credit, debit, and deficit. Learners may need significant practice in different forms of accounting, book-keeping, or stock-taking before working on the real thing.

Farmers in Senegal were introduced to the value of book-keeping by working first on personal account sheets. These were record sheets kept by individuals, listing hours worked in their field and any money spent on their crop. The number of sacks harvested and any money gained from selling produce were recorded on the same sheet. Learners were introduced to the idea over a season, and had weekly practice in filling in the sheet. By the end of the season, they had sufficient skills to calculate their profits and their losses.

The results of the end-of-year calculations showed the amount of time and the costs incurred in cultivating different crops. They also showed the relative profits and yields involved. Comparisons could be made between different agricultural practices used by different group members. Farmers could see for themselves whether the inputs involved in, for example, irrigated agriculture were justified by the yield, and estimate the risks they had taken when investing money in fertiliser or pesticide. Recording the amount of money spent on the cultivation of a particular crop helped them to make decisions about what to cultivate the following year, and what and when to sell. The fluctuating price of grain indicated whether investing money in storing produce and selling later made good economic sense. The exercise gave the learners not only practice in the number skills used in accounting, but greater insight into the uses and value of book-keeping. By calculating actual and possible profits and losses, they were able to make more informed choices about how much to spend on inputs, and assess the need for paying into an insurance fund.

Figure 6.4:
A basic accounts sheet used by farmers in Senegal (translated from Pulaar)

Individual record sheet

Name _____ **Crop** _____

Date	Hours of work	Expenses	Sacks harvested	Sacks sold	Income

Reading images

It is often wrongly assumed that people without literacy skills will understand pictures or photographs. While this may be true for those who have grown up in an urban environment, where advertising boards and magazines are common, it is not always true for the villager. But using literacy will generally mean encountering images, pictures, or ideograms at some stage. Newspapers, catalogues, information leaflets, and advertising material all use pictures and written text alternately. Some literacy primers are based on using words to accompany pictures; but it is a mistake to assume that the pictures will be understood automatically: it may be necessary to introduce the reading of pictures first. This skill includes understanding several crucial facts:

- that the marks made on the page represent something which is probably much larger than the image;
- that pictures tend to translate an outline shape into two dimensions;
- that, while writing is read in a pre-defined direction (left to right, right to left, or top to bottom), pictures are read by looking at the whole image at once.

Village people gain their knowledge through handling, creating, or looking at actual objects or events. When they see a picture, they expect it to contain what they know about the object and not only what they see of the object. A photograph or drawing of a man in which only one leg and one arm is visible will not necessarily be recognised as a man. A drawing of a truck in which only two wheels can be seen will not correspond to what people know about trucks. In an image which shows perspective, two objects of the same size, one farther away than the other, may be perceived as two objects of different sizes. (See Figure 6.5.)

Artists preparing pictures for new learners need to bear such problems of perception in mind, and take care to represent what the learners expect to see. It should be remembered that pictures which contain shading and foreshortening may be read literally: the person may be seen to have a scarred face or a short limb, or lack the limbs which are not visible. (See Figure 6.6.)

Learners need to be introduced to images and taught to read and interpret them, just as they are introduced to words. Pictures should be discussed, comparing what the learner sees with what the image-maker might have intended. Even a simplified drawing, such as Figure 6.7, may rely on conventions which a skilled reader would take for granted — in this case, the use of an arrow to indicate direction.

Advertising campaigns often use non-realistic images, enlarging areas of the picture for effect. This is often the case in anti-malarial health campaigns, where mosquitoes are enlarged to make them more easily recognised. New learners are more likely to interpret such an image literally and fail to recognise a giant mosquito as anything they are likely to come into contact with. In the case of the pesticide advertisement in

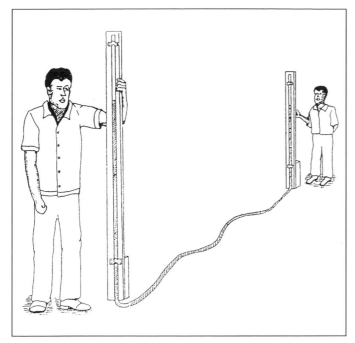

Figure 6.5: Measuring contour-lines: will the exaggerated perspective distract attention from the technique?

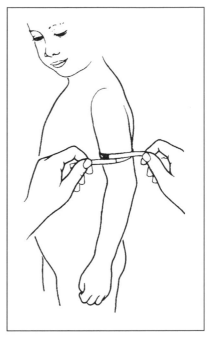

Figure 6.6: Measuring mid-upper arm circumference: will the child be seen as having only one arm?

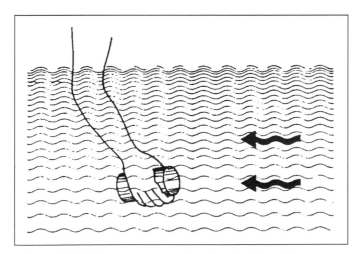

Figure 6.7: Taking a water sample against the flow of the current: will the arrows be read literally by learners unfamiliar with this convention?

Figure 6.8: Pesticide advertisement: will farmers identify the giant beetle as a real threat?

Figure 6.8, it is open to question whether farmers will identify the giant insect as a real threat, or even identify themselves with the stylised depiction of a farmer.

Technical advisers such as agricultural engineers may make use of cross-sectional diagrams in drawing irrigation canals or construction diagrams. Mechanics may need to understand a diagram of a tractor engine or a motor pump. If learners are introduced to the conventions used in these diagrams, and taught to interpret them, the drawings can be a useful tool in future learning. (See Figure 6.9.)

Figure 6.9: Cross-section of a well, carrying vital information, but requiring sophisticated skills of interpretation

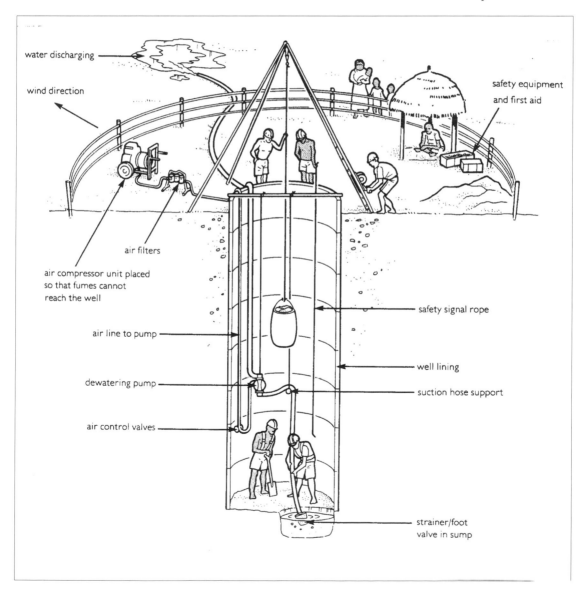

water discharging

wind direction

safety equipment and first aid

air filters

air compressor unit placed so that fumes cannot reach the well

safety signal rope

air line to pump

well lining

suction hose support

dewatering pump

air control valves

strainer/foot valve in sump

Learners will already have their own way of representing objects that are familiar to them. In helping them to interpret unfamiliar pictures, it is useful to start with their own pictures. Every culture has its own way of representing concrete things in two dimensions. Learners should be encouraged to bring examples from their own local culture to share with the literacy group. It would be even more interesting to encourage them to draw their own: this will mean that the group will have to work out together how to represent such features as distance and perspective.

Reading maps

Development workers, beginning to work in an area for the first time, often ask community members to draw a map of their village. This process helps to give the worker an 'insider's' view of a community, and an indication of the relative importance of individual people, buildings, or places within the village. When asked to present a picture of their village, people will generally draw in the important places largest, or first. But remember that the concept of translating a large area into a small, two-dimensional representation of that area may be new in some cultures, and handled differently in others.

The exercise of asking people to map their village is valuable on many levels. It challenges them to think about how to make visual representations. It begins to introduce the idea of two-dimensional drawing and of scale. It is a useful first step from which to move on to maps of an area, region, country, or continent.

When introducing people to maps, it is helpful to bear in mind the following guidelines:

- Start small: begin with their own representation of their village, or part of a village.

- Introduce new roads or buildings gradually, relating them to what people already know.

- Build up from this, by adding on adjoining villages, and then showing a whole region.

- Whatever maps are introduced, always start by putting in the places which people know, and relating other places to the named locations.

Remember that a map is a complex visual picture, and reading it requires a lot of skill.

CHAPTER 7

Planning a session

Setting goals

While the general aims of a literacy programme will be decided on by the learners at the beginning (see Chapter 3), a plan and specific goals also need to be set for each session. This involves thinking in advance about the best way to spend the time together, and having some idea of what should be achieved by the end of it.

Some literacy workers follow a tightly structured plan with clear goals. The danger of this is that what they intend to teach may become more important than what is actually learned. They may stick rigidly to their plans, regardless of whether or not the learners are interested, involved, or clear about what is happening. Working in this way may make the literacy worker feel good, but it is of less value to the learners.

Other literacy workers completely disregard the need for a session plan, and wait for the learners to decide how to spend the time. While this may be effective when working with individuals, it is much more difficult with a group. Discussions can move without purpose between unrelated bits of information, and the learners may be left wondering what they have learned. Having invested a lot of effort in making time for the session, they will soon lose motivation or their confidence in the authority of the literacy worker.

It is generally helpful to decide in advance on goals for a session. This means thinking about what would be useful for the learners and what could be realistically achieved in the time available. Once goals are set, literacy workers can outline the various steps and activities that will enable learners to reach them. They can also ensure that they have the tools and materials necessary to cover these steps. A good session plan consists of

- clear goals;
- an outline of the steps and activities to reach them;
- the approximate time the activities will take;
- a list of necessary materials.

A good plan will also leave time to review things learned in the previous session, to discuss areas of particular importance to the learners, and to look forward to what might be achieved during the following session.

Some examples of **goals** set in advance might include

- understanding the headlines and main information from a newspaper story;
- recognising and writing the most important place names from the story, and finding them on a map of the town.

Steps to achieve them might include

- recognising letters/words/syllables from the headlines;
- predicting the content of the story;
- discussing with the group their knowledge of the event;
- working in small groups to find familiar words in the story;
- following the text, while the literacy worker reads the story;
- choosing the place names that are useful and writing them;
- identifying familiar places on a map;
- locating new place names on the map.

Materials needed will include

- newspaper headlines written large enough for everyone to see, perhaps on a chalk board;
- one copy of the newspaper story for each small group;
- pencil and paper for each learner;
- a large map;
- possibly smaller copies of the map for each group to work on.

Setting goals and outlining a session plan generally help to give a literacy worker confidence. But a plan should never be so rigid that it cannot be changed if it seems not to be working, or if something more important arises. Learners will have their own goals, which will change regularly; things will come up which they may prefer to discuss; activities may need to be abandoned, if time runs out.

Learners are always more important than session plans, but a session with no goals may not get anywhere at all.

Writing a session plan

People learn best when they are active rather than passive. A range of learning activities should help learners to exercise and build on the understanding they already have, in order to discover new things, and to practise and improve upon their skills. But it is difficult for people to concentrate for long periods of time on one thing. A session plan should try to change the activity about every twenty minutes, and to shift the focus from activities which are led by the literacy worker to those which entail people working alone or with each other.

A plan for the session just described might look like this:

Goals: Understanding a story; identifying individual words; copying words; using a map.

Steps: Reading headlines; predicting story; understanding story; finding individual words; writing place names; locating these on a map.

Materials: A copy of the story for each group; a large map; a small map; cards with place names written on them.

Time	Activity	Notes
18.00	Present headlines to group. Group identify familiar letters/syllables/words. Read headlines.	Write on board in advance.
18.15	Small-group discussion of the story. Relate back to whole group.	In groups of 3?
18.35	Read story, learners follow text.	Give out copies. Trace in the air and then copy in books.
18.45	Discussion as whole group of events in text.	
19.00	In pairs, finding place names in texts.	
19.15	Write up place names; learners copy.	
19.35	Introduce group to map. Individuals identify places.	Put up large map.
19.45	Give out copy of maps; in pairs: how many places can each pair read/recognise?	
20.00	Add new place names to map.	Learners write without copying.

Working in small groups

Certain learning activities are designed to be carried out in small groups and without a literacy worker. Besides providing a change of activity and a shift of focus, they encourage independence in the learners and give them an opportunity to work out something for themselves. Generally it means learners doing things at their own pace, rather than listening to the literacy worker or moving at the pace of the whole group.

Groups become autonomous: people working in pairs, or in threes or fours, have the chance to reflect on their experience, to listen to that of others, and to use that experience to make decisions. Working like this, without a leader, presents the learners with a challenge. If the challenge is demanding or exciting, the learners are more likely to be fully involved and active in solving it. Such a task demands that they use their creativity to find the answer to a series of problems. They are required to think for

People generally learn best when they are solving problems in small groups — like these men, teaching themselves English in a refugee camp in Somalia.
Photo: Jeremy Hartley

themselves, to discuss and to work together. Most people learn best in this way. When they are fully involved, they are working at their hardest, and more learning is taking place.

The literacy worker may need to intervene to form or change the groups and encourage members to work together. If groups are working on a problem, then everyone in the group needs to be involved. If decisions are made by the group, then every member needs to understand what is happening. If everyone is to learn, then it is important for all group members to listen to each other and respect each other's ideas, regardless of their value, and regardless of the differences of class, caste, or age which may operate outside the learning situation.

While the groups are working on the set task, it is the responsibility of the literacy worker to keep track of the time. When the tasks have been completed, the literacy worker should bring the whole group together again, to check their results against each other's. It is important to value everyone's contribution. A worker who merely provides the 'correct' answer, without discussion, devalues the work which learners have put into the task. Time should be spent analysing and discussing, and discovering how different groups arrived at different solutions. *It is the process of learning, rather than the result, which has the most value.*

Some guidelines for small-group work

- Respect the learners; try to see things from their point of view.
- Encourage a friendly, relaxed working environment.
- Don't give explanations: ask questions.
- Try to ask open questions; for example: *What do you think about ... How did you ... How would you ...?* These are better than questions that need

one-word answers, such as *Would you ... Did you ...?*

- Give clear instructions to the learners. Make sure they know what they are doing and why they are doing it.
- Give learners an idea of how long they will have to complete the task.
- Try to vary the composition of the groups and encourage people to work with everyone at some time; this will help to prevent the same people dominating each small group.
- Small-group work is a time for the literacy worker to take a back seat. Give clear instructions and then move away from the centre of the room.
- Keep in touch with the progress of each group; listen in to discussions; be available to clarify the task if the groups need it.

Some basic learning activities

Reading in pairs

This is a reading exercise which uses stronger readers to help less fluent readers. It can also be done by a literacy worker and a learner. It involves reading aloud, but in a way which gives expression to the *meaning* of a text, rather than encouraging straight repetition. It helps learners to read fluently and increase their reading speeds.

1 The stronger reader reads the text aloud, with expression, at a normal speed.

2 The stronger reader reads the text again, more slowly, giving the learner a chance to follow the words in the text as they are read. This is repeated as many times as necessary.

3 The learner reads the text, with the stronger reader following the words. The learner should read as slowly as she or he needs to at first.

4 By following the learners as they read, it is possible to notice the words they stumble over, and those they read fluently. It will also show the strategies they use for reading: whether they approach a difficult word by sounding it out, or by guessing according to the context. It will show whether or not the learners understand the meaning of the text as they read, and whether they are able to read it in a way that makes 'sense'.

The stronger reader is able to help the other learner with difficult words. By occasionally joining in, the stronger reader can gradually speed up the other's pace, and help him or her to read with expression and confidence. However, it may take many readings of the text before they are able to do this.

Reading in pairs follows some cultural conventions of reading aloud, but encourages the learners to give meaning to what they read. This technique should be used with care in areas where people are reluctant to read in front of others.

Sentence/word matching

This is a good activity for new learners. It encourages them to look carefully at the shapes made by letters.

1 Write down a sentence in letters several centimetres high on a blank sheet of paper.

The bank in Podor opens at 11 o'clock

2 Write the same sentence again, this time using a small piece of card for each new word.

The | bank | in | Podor | opens | at | 11 | o'clock

3 Read the sentence aloud to the learners several times, then give each of them one of the individual word-cards.

4 Ask them to place 'their' words on top of the same words in the complete sentence; this requires learners to recognise what the word looks like and match it up.

5 When all the word-cards have been placed on top of the sentence, read it aloud again, pointing to the individual words as they are read.

6 Ask the learners to find a certain word. If this is difficult for them, read the sentence aloud again, pointing to the words as they are read. Continue to do this until the learners are able to identify a word when it is said on its own.

7 Later, when the learners are more confident, they can be asked to find individual words from the cards, without using the complete sentence to match them against.

This activity can be done with individuals or groups. If you use sentences suggested by the learners, it helps to ensure that the words which are learned are useful. Once sentences have been learned, they should be kept and used again later for revision.

As the learners become more experienced, they can use individual words from different sentences to make new sentences. Similarly, they can be given a sentence with words written on individual cards, but in the wrong order, and asked to sort it out.

bank | Podor | 11 | The | opens | in | o'clock | at

This activity can be converted into a writing exercise by asking learners to choose one of the words and identify the different letters in it. Letters too can be placed in the wrong order for the learners to sort out. Sorting letters is a much more difficult exercise, and should be attempted only with words with a small number of letters.

When learners have become confident in recognising an individual word and some of the letters in it, they can begin to try writing it. They may need to do this first by copying or tracing (see below).

Sentences with beads or sticks

A similar exercise, for more experienced readers, can be carried out using beads to represent individual words. Learners suggest sentences, which the literacy worker represents by using beads or sticks of an appropriate length for individual words. The learners then try to write the words alone or in groups. It is a more meaningful exercise than a spelling test given from a list of words. Representing words in this way encourages learners to focus on one word at a time, and to leave a space for those they cannot spell.

1 Suggest a sentence and say it aloud, or ask one of the learners to choose a sentence which they would like to be able to write.

2 Say it aloud a couple of times, and then repeat each word in order individually, placing a new bead down in front of the learners for each new word (a small bead for a short word, larger ones for longer words). This will serve to remind learners of the breaks between words, and the number of words in a given sentence.

3 Ask the learners to repeat the sentence aloud, pointing to the individual beads as they go.

4 Now ask them to write as many of the words as they are able, and to leave gaps for the ones they cannot write.

This exercise can be done with individuals, with a group, or in pairs. If a number of pairs are competing against each other, it can become a game. Once the learners have written as many words as they are able, they can check the answers with each other and correct them; then new words can be taught. The exercise can also be used by the literacy worker to see how much the learners have remembered from earlier classes.

Finding the important words

This exercise encourages learners to listen for meaning and then to find certain words in a written text.

1   Read a text aloud to the learners.

2   Ask them what the text was about.

3   Ask them to suggest the words which they think are important in the text which they have heard.

4   Give them the text to look through, and ask them to find the words they have suggested. This can be made easier by telling them the line on which they can find each word.

5   When they have found the word, they can try to write it, first by copying and later from memory.

Asking learners to look for certain words in a text introduces them to skim reading: to the idea that they need not read every word in order to find the one they are looking for. Much reading takes place in this way. Looking for information (in a telephone directory, for example) or looking through a longer text to find a specific piece of information (such as the name of the politician involved in a newspaper story) are examples of skimming through a text. Learners should be introduced to the value of this early on, and not feel it is always necessary to read every single word.

This exercise can be used with texts in different type-sizes and different lay-outs, such as lists, continuous writing, and tables. As learners progress, they may need to recognise and use different ways of presenting similar information themselves.

Tracing letters and words

New readers sometimes find it easier to trace a letter or word before trying to write it. Individual letters can be traced in the air, as well as on paper. It has been suggested that making the letter large and tracing it with wide arm movements helps to fix the shape of it in a learner's mind. When working on paper, it is important to start with the letter or word written large enough for learners to trace it, first with their fingers on top of the written word; they can then build up to writing it, by tracing first in pencil on top of the written word, and then copying it underneath, before writing it independently.

As with all these exercises, different learners will progress through them at different speeds. Some learners will need to repeat each stage a number of times before they have the confidence to move on. Other learners may move quickly and then need to go back over the earlier steps on another occasion. People learn in different ways and at different speeds, and their learning styles should be respected.

Searching for answers

This is an exercise for more experienced learners. It encourages them to read for meaning and to do something with the information they read. Students are presented with a written text, and with a number of questions about that text. The exercise can be done with individuals or with groups, using a text that has been written by one of the learners, or by one from outside. However, the information which learners are asked to look for needs to be relevant and useful to them. It could, for example, be a way of dealing with health information or agricultural extension material.

Presenting learners with written information, and asking them to search for answers to specific questions, alone or in groups, begins to introduce them to the practical value of the skills they are learning. For some learners it may be the first time they have tried to solve problems by using written information, rather than by asking someone or by trying it out for themselves. However, it is important to encourage learners to question and debate the information that is written down, rather than to accept it unquestioningly. In many cultures, the written word is thought to carry great power. A literacy worker needs to be aware of the status which learners accord to written information; this would be a fruitful subject for group discussion.

Problem-solving in pyramids

Problem-solving is an important approach to learning literacy and numeracy skills and encouraging learners to deal with new information co-operatively, without the help of a literacy worker. By breaking up the problem into different steps, it can become a group activity in which learners are able to check their answers with each other as they go.

A 'pyramid' approach starts small and expands: at each stage of the activity, the group of problem-solvers gets bigger. This is often a good way to generate ideas. It gives individuals a chance to reflect on their own, share their ideas with someone else, and then debate them with another group who have followed the same process. As the group grows, so does the issue which they are discussing. This encourages people to report the decisions they have made, justify them, and reach agreement in order to tackle the next question.

1 Ask the group to think about the first stage of a problem on their own: *The members of an agricultural co-operative are paying money into a sinking fund, to replace a motor pump. Where could they keep the money while they are saving?*

2 Ask them then to discuss this with one other person and agree on a realistic answer. Then give them the second set of questions to sort out together: *A savings account at a bank would earn interest at five per cent a year. If the ten members of the co-operative contributed 300 francs each in the first year, how much interest would they get? How much money would they have in total?*

3 When the pair have had time to discuss this, ask them to work with another pair to compare answers among the four of them. They should try to agree on a realistic plan. Give them the next part of the problem: *How long would it take the group to save the 25,000 francs needed for a new pump? How much interest would be earned over this time?*

93

4 Finally they can join together as a whole group and discuss the advantages and disadvantages of a bank account, and compare it with other ways of saving money.

Groups may not be able to reach agreement. It is important for the literacy worker to be aware of what is happening, and if necessary move them on. The whole activity can collapse if individuals are in conflict with each other.

Filling the gaps

Providing learners with a story or piece of writing in which certain words have been left out is a good exercise in the skills of reading, understanding, writing, and spelling. It provides practice in all these skills, and can also be used as a testing device. Gap-fill exercises can be based on a learner's own writing, or a specially written story, or an article that learners have already read. The words which are blanked out can be either those that need particular practice, or words which occur at regular intervals (every ninth word, for example). The latter is called a 'Cloze' exercise (although this word is often incorrectly used for any gap-fill exercise). It involves learners in practising a range of different words and encourages them to read fluently and anticipate the missing words.

The easiest way to prepare a gap-fill exercise is to use a copy of the complete text and to cut out or white out the words, leaving a space. Using dashes to indicate the number of letters in the missing word makes the exercise slightly easier:

The women gathered together for a meeting in the ---- centre.

Story-telling

Most oral cultures record history and communicate events through story-telling, and teach moral and cultural values through riddles and proverbs. Story-tellers are often professional in their craft, and stories and legends that have been passed down between generations form part of the common knowledge of a community.

Stories can be used in a literacy class in a number of ways:

- Tell a story and ask learners to write the ending.
- Tell a story first and then read it together.
- Encourage learners to tell a story using beads or stones to represent the main events, and then ask the group to write it down.
- Tell a story to generate discussion about a particular topic or event.
- Tell a story to illustrate a point about teaching or learning, particularly to groups of trainee literacy workers.
- Use a tape recorder to record village story-tellers; transcribe some of the stories over time to contribute to a village library.

Recognising large numbers

Recognising large numbers is always difficult, but particularly so for new learners. Short bursts of regular practice in reading large numbers aloud will help. One way to do this is to build up the number, naming it as each new digit is added.

1 Write up a single-figure number and ask the learners to say it aloud: 7.
2 Add another figure to the left of the number and ask the learners to say it aloud: 27.
3 Add another figure to the left of the number: 327.
4 Go on adding numbers to make the whole number grow: 4,327, 64,327, 564,327, 8,564,327, 98,564,327 ... up to the largest number that learners can confidently deal with.

This game can be extended by adding numbers after a decimal point.

Bingo

This is another game which practises number recognition. Give out cards with different numbers written on them in a series of boxes. One person selects numbers at random from another pack of cards which have a single number on each card, and calls them out. Players who can find the number on their card mark it off or cover it over. The first player with all numbers covered is the winner, and should shout out something to claim the victory. The winning player's numbers then need to be checked against those that have actually been called.

Arranging the numbers on cards with spaces in between makes them easier to read. Placing them out of numerical order makes recognition more difficult and the game more challenging. (See Figure 7.1.)

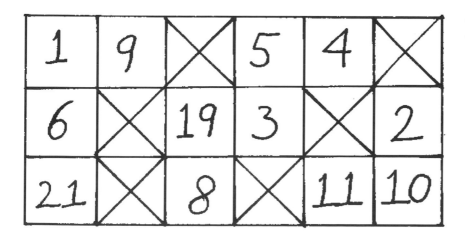

Figure 7.1:
A bingo card

Board games

Board games in which learners throw a dice and move a counter across a board also provide good practice in number recognition and addition: each time a new number is thrown, it is added to the player's existing score.

Board games can be made more interesting by building in penalties and advantages. This can be easily done by marking out certain squares where, if players fall on them, they have to pick up a card and answer a question. This adds practice in literacy skills and local knowledge or technical information to the game. If the answer is correct, the player can progress; if it is wrong, he or she goes back to the beginning or misses a turn. Questions will need to be changed regularly; but, once a board has been drawn up, it can be used with many different question packs.

A board game can become a competition if a group of learners is divided into two teams. When one team falls on the question square, the other team asks the question.

Some dice use a series of dots to indicate the numbers on each of the six faces. A dice that uses figures instead of dots is more useful for practising number recognition. Board games can be played with two dice, instead of the usual one. Learners can add, multiply, or subtract the numbers on the dice, to arrive at the number of squares which they should move.

Figure 7.2:
A simple board game

Board games can be used to practise more than one skill at a time, if the literacy worker is inventive enough. Are there any existing local games that might be adapted or used for practising number or letter skills?

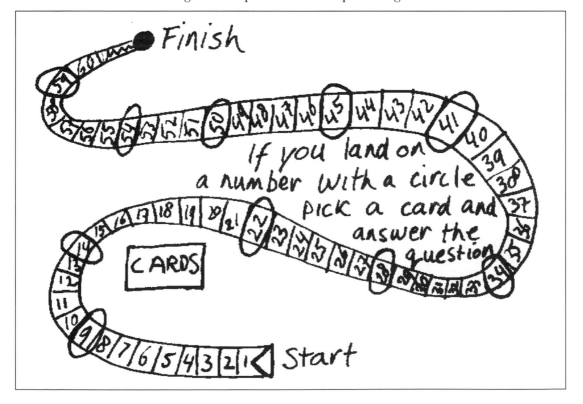

CHAPTER 8

Selecting and training literacy workers

Choosing people to be trained as literacy workers is never an easy task. It generally involves weighing up factors such as popularity; an ability to deal with people; fluency in reading and writing in the language of literacy; and a person's commitment, motivation, and availability. Remember that people can be trained to teach things like grammar or multiplication, but the ability to deal sensitively with people takes much longer to acquire.

The role of a literacy worker

The task of a literacy worker is not to hand out knowledge to people who will absorb it without question. Nor are they in any sense superior to those who are learning. They are adults working with other adults, who have already learned many things in their lives. Literacy workers may have different experiences and different knowledge from the other people in their groups. About some things they will know more; about others, less. Their task is to help the group to discover and discuss the things they want to know about, and to practise the skills they want to acquire. Their role is very different from that of the traditional school teacher.

A traditional teacher	A good literacy worker
Gives information to a class.	Helps the group to discover what they want to know.
Expects the group to be passive.	Expects the group to be active.
Asks for obedience.	Asks for trust.
Sees students as people needing help.	Sees students as equals.
Talks down to students.	Encourages students to share information with each other.
Passes on recognised knowledge.	Challenges recognised knowledge.
Views the world from his/her own perspective.	Tries to see things from the students' perspective.
Makes decisions and tells the group.	Makes decisions with the group.

Selecting literacy workers for training

Here are some guidelines to bear in mind when considering whom to train for literacy work.

- Do they have experience as well as knowledge of literacy and numeracy skills? Consider not only whether they *can* read, but whether they *do* read. Find out not only whether they *can* keep accounts, but whether they *do* keep accounts, or have done so recently. It is experience rather than knowledge alone that enables someone to talk about something with confidence, and share the reality of how to do it with others.

- Can they communicate their experience? Do they share the same first language as their group, or can they speak it fluently? Do they have experience of a similar cultural background? Can they relate easily to group members?

  It has often been found that people from a nearby area, rather than the immediate area where the learners live, make better leaders. It may be hard for a community to accept someone they have known since childhood; but a complete outsider will not have the advantage of sharing a similar cultural background and common understanding of the world, and will not be able to use real-life examples convincingly.

- Are they acceptable to the group? Will the person in question be seen by the group as someone they can identify with and respect? (Factors of age and sex may be particularly important in certain groups.)

- Are they likely to stay in the area? A learning programme may be interrupted or ended if literacy workers move away from the area,

Literacy class for tree-nursery workers, Tigray, Ethiopia.
In some cultures, men may not be accustomed to seeing women in the role of teacher.
Photo: Jenny Matthews

even for short periods. Investment in training group leaders may be wasted if they are unable to continue with their work.

- Are they open to learning new ways of doing things? A good literacy worker will need to hold regular reviews of the group's progress, and respond to comments from group members and colleagues. Initial training in running groups before a worker undertakes this role, and supportive training while the programme is running, are both very important.

  It is often easier to train someone who has never done any teaching before than to re-train a primary-school teacher. Primary-school teachers will already have fixed ways of working with groups that are more appropriate to children than adults. Many find it difficult to change.

- Are they committed and enthusiastic? Formal educational qualifications are not necessarily the mark of a good literacy worker. Someone who has a high level of formal education may find it difficult to understand the needs and realities of someone wanting to learn literacy skills. They may also see themselves as superior.

  It has been found that people trained as literacy workers to work in a non-formal way still slip back into teaching others in the way that they were taught. Someone who has spent a lot of time in formal schooling may find themselves taking on the role of a traditional school teacher almost unconsciously. This is generally inappropriate to an adult literacy class. Someone who is committed to the people in the group and enthusiastic about learning to work with them will probably make a far better group leader.

Selecting visiting tutors

The group may decide to invite visitors to come in from time to time and work with them on specific topics. Visiting tutors may be selected more for their specialist areas of knowledge than for their personal qualities.

- Beware of people who will overload the group with unnecessary information, or speak in technical or abstract language that they will find difficult to understand. This is a waste of time, and can harm the confidence of group members who are beginning to learn new skills. They may be discouraged or made to feel stupid.

- Try to select people who will be sympathetic to the needs of the group. Look for people who will be open to answering questions from group members and exploring the areas that they are interested in.

- Beware of people who are more interested in showing what they know than in finding out what the group wants to know.

- Offer advice to help the visitor plan how much information to cover in the time available, and how to apportion the time.

- Ask the group in advance to give suggestions about the sort of information they would find useful, and pass this on to the visiting tutor.

Learning on site

Arranging for the group to visit specialist informants in their work-places may be more useful than inviting specialists to visit the group. It enables the students to see people working in their own environments and to get a more realistic picture of what they do. It may also give students the chance to try out some of their new skills in a real context, instead of the rather artificial situations created within the class.

For example, groups learning to maintain and repair a motor pump and to keep accounts for it might meet a mechanic in a workshop or in the field. Here they would be able to get some hands-on experience of taking a pump apart and putting it together again. Even those who would not be directly responsible for maintenance would get useful insights into why and how a pump used the fuel which they were accounting for. It would make accounting seem less abstract and more related to real things. People find it easier to learn things that are real and meaningful to them than to remember abstract and unrelated ideas.

Groups learning about how a bank functions might visit a cashier in the bank. This would give them the chance to see and use the various forms available, and to learn some of the social conventions associated with using a bank. Many of them may never have been inside a bank before. It would enable them to find out where it was, and would help to break down barriers to an unfamiliar environment.

Specialist informants and group visits are likely to be most useful once there has been some basic literacy learning, and the group are ready to move on to new things.

Training literacy workers

Much has been written about preparing adults to work with other adults as learners. Development workers themselves will have been trained to communicate with adults from their own culture and from other cultures and to work with individuals and with groups. Many of these strategies can be adapted for work in literacy. This book aims to give only some general guidelines on how training for literacy workers might be organised, and ideas about what has happened in other small programmes.

Training can be organised at different stages:

1 **Initial training**, before the literacy programme starts: to give workers confidence and help to prepare them to plan a session and manage a group.

2 **In-service training**, while they are acting as literacy workers: to offer support and to give them the chance to discuss how things are going, to look at what is working well, and to analyse problems.

3 **Reflection**, after a period of acting as a literacy worker: to give a chance to reflect on how things have gone, to question whether the aims set by the group have been met, and to learn from the experience; to plan where to go from here.

If the training is to involve a number of literacy workers, the opportunity to exchange fears, ideas, and experiences among themselves has as much value as any suggestions offered by outsiders. Time should be made available for this.

The training programme itself can be a valuable example of alternative ways of working with adults. It can provide a different model from the one which students experienced at school, and offer one which literacy workers might use as a basis for their own classes. Time should be made available to reflect on the *process* as well as the content of initial training.

In order for group leaders to develop confidence in running groups, the programme should provide a 'practice time' in which new leaders try out their skills by teaching each other. Watching other people teaching, and giving and receiving comments on how someone leads a class, is a very effective way in which to develop skills.

It is important that the values and principles which are to be introduced into a literacy programme are present in the training programme for group leaders. Both programmes should value the contributions of participants, and should encourage active learning, self-discovery, and reflection. The group leaders themselves should play an active part in deciding what would be good practice when working with their own groups in the future.

The programme outlined below suggests questions which can be used to begin each session. They are designed to encourage the literacy workers to reflect on their own past experience and to discuss it together. Their discussions will form the basis for new learning.

Further information on some of the areas covered in the training programme can be found in other parts of this chapter and in the next one.

In Senegal, initial training of literacy workers was offered in two five-day workshops. This was felt to be the maximum amount of time that people could spend away from their families. After this, the group leaders met for two days every other month (one weekend every eight weeks). When their first year as group leaders was over, they met for a further five days together, to review progress and plan for the following year.

In a Nepali literacy programme where VSO volunteers have worked, literacy tutors were mainly young, unmarried girls, and the training course was an intensive 35-day residential period. However, a part of this involved working through the content of literacy primers with trainee tutors, and refreshing and upgrading their own literacy skills.

An example of a training programme for group leaders

(supplied by a VSO volunteer from Nepal)

Initial Training Programme: Part 1 (5/6 days)

Day 1 (arrival)
Session 1: evening session (2 hours)
What is learning? How do adults learn? How do children learn? What are the differences? Participants think about good and bad learning experiences in their own lives, from childhood to adulthood, and discuss these in small groups. What conclusions can be drawn from this about how adults learn best? How generalised are these conclusions? Can they be applied to literacy groups? *[See Part One of this book.]*

Day 2
Session 2: morning session (3 hours)
What is literacy and why do students want it? How do people perceive literacy locally? Is there a difference between numeracy and literacy? Do they always go together? What do students want to learn? Why do they want to learn it? How can group leaders find out? How can they check that they have got it right? *[See Part Two of this book.]*

Session 3: afternoon session (3 hours)
How did you learn to read? Participants reflect on their own experience of learning to read, and try to identify the different strategies used. Which of these strategies might be appropriate to adults, and why? How much will students be able to read already? How can you find this out?
  Further approaches to teaching reading. *[See Chapter 5 of this book.]*

Session 4: evening session (2 hours)
Practical session: assessing a range of reading materials, and considering how to use them in a literacy programme.

Day 3
Session 5: morning session (3 hours)
How did you learn to write? Did you learn to write and to read at the same time? Are reading and writing two separate activities? Do you need to learn one first? If so, which one? Should they be learned together? Which approaches to teaching writing might be most appropriate to adults in

your area? Can students write anything already? How can you find this out? What should your starting point be in your classes?

Further approaches to teaching writing. *[See Chapter 5 of this book.]*

Session 6: afternoon session (3 hours)
Working with numbers. What records do people keep in the area where the literacy programme will be held? How is this information recorded? How do people calculate? How familiar are they with the concept of numbers? What number system will you introduce them to in the context of the literacy class? How can this be related to what they know already? How can you establish what they know already? How much do they need to know, and in what order should they learn it? Which learning activities can be used for introducing and working with numbers? *[See Chapter 6 of this book.]*

Session 7: evening session (2 hours)
Practical/social session, meeting development workers from other programmes. How can literacy contribute to other fields of development work?

Day 4
Session 8: morning session (3 hours)
Planning a session, establishing aims and goals, and writing a session plan. *[See Chapter 7 of this book.]*

Session 9: afternoon session (3 hours)
Bringing it all together to work on real tasks. Identifying the tasks for which people will need literacy in the area where the programme will be held. Working with words, numbers, images to deal with some of these situations.

Session 10: evening session (2 hours)
Setting up practice-teaching session for the following day. Giving individuals a subject or a topic to work with and practical help during planning time.

Day 5
Session 11: morning session (3 hours)
Practice-teaching sessions

Session 12: afternoon session (3 hours)
Practice-teaching sessions

Session 13: evening session (2 hours)
Social event; ways of staying in touch and supporting each other in the months ahead.

Day 6
Session 14: morning session (3 hours)
Discussing and evaluating strategies used during this training

programme. Thinking about the importance of evaluation, and when and how to evaluate. *[See Chapter 9 of this book.]*

Afternoon: Planning second training session.

Departure

Initial Training Programme: Part 2 (5 days)

To include:

Revision of areas covered in Part 1.
Using materials already available for literacy. *[See Chapter 11 of this book.]*
Developing new materials for literacy. *[See Chapter 10 of this book.]*
Assessing learning.
Practice-teaching sessions.

Practice sessions

During practice sessions, each trainee will have the opportunity to try leading a group, while the others act as literacy students. This allows everyone to try out different ways of setting up a discussion or presenting information, and also to experience these as a student. Comments given after the session can draw attention to things that should be developed and those which should be changed. The practice sessions need to be a positive experience, which builds confidence and offers constructive lessons to everyone.

Guidelines for practice sessions

- The first practice sessions should not be too long (10–20 minutes). Trainees can gradually build up to leading longer sessions.

- The aims of each practice session should be made clear in advance to the person leading it; for example: *introduce the group to simple addition and give a few examples*.

- The person preparing the session should be allowed time and support in deciding, for example, in what sequence to introduce things, and what to 'tell' the group and what to let them try out for themselves.

- Before hearing comments from the group, leaders should be given a chance to comment on their session themselves. ('I don't think I started off very well: I was quite nervous at the beginning and thought I was talking too fast.')

- Comments from the group should, as far as possible, begin and end on a positive note, with constructive criticism in between. ('I liked the way you smiled when you started, and looked at everyone. I got a bit confused when you were talking about numbers: you were writing on the board and I couldn't hear you properly. Your work on the board was very clear, though.')

- Comments should be as specific as possible, and concerned with aspects of teaching practice that might actually be changed. ('The session dragged a bit when you were explaining addition, and you could have done that part more quickly'; not 'I found it boring'!)

- Comments could be organised around a checklist of 'things to look for'; for example:

Blackboard: Is the writing large enough for everyone to see? Are the words used on the board readable by the class? Is the information on the board well organised?

Voice: Can the group hear everything that is said? Does the worker face the group when he or she is talking? Does the worker look at the people in the group? Does he or she speak too fast or too slowly?

Questions: Did the worker ask questions of everyone in the group? Were students given a chance to talk through their own ideas?

Information: Was the information given clear? Did the worker stay with the aim set for the class?

Conclusion

Throughout this book, we have stressed the key role of the literacy worker in forming good working relationships with learners. We have encouraged workers to be innovative and creative. We have suggested that programmes should be designed with and for the target groups, rather than by professionals working outside the community, standard-ising programmes for a whole country. We have indicated that, if primers are used, they might be better used critically and selectively, rather than followed as a set format for every class.

All this gives literacy workers more control, and therefore more responsibility. So it is vital they they understand and support the philosophy behind participatory work. To succeed, they will need the confidence to experiment and to take risks, to think on their feet and respond spontaneously to learners' questions. They must be able to take control when appropriate, but also feel comfortable about sitting back and letting learners work independently.

Some of these skills are acquired with experience, but new workers will need courage and self-confidence not to be defeated when things get tough. Training programmes should help them to explore their attitutes towards learners and ways of learning, as well as giving them practice sessions and supportive feedback. They will need initial training in practical skills, but just as important are regular meetings to review progress and deal with individual problems.

CHAPTER 9

Assessing progress and evaluating impact

Assessment should not be a very complicated matter. Assessing learning and teaching involves planning activities which will help us to find out what has been happening. What is being achieved? What changes are occurring? Are good things happening? Are there aspects that need to be improved?

In Chapter 4, we suggested that some time and thought should be given to planning for assessment. What is its purpose? Who is it for? Who will do it? and so on. In this chapter we will look at approaches to assessment in more detail. Many of the ideas offered in Chapter 5, on teaching methods, can also be used for assessment. Using some of the same methods for teaching and assessment will help to make assessment an integral part of the learning process.

Participative assessment

Adults learn best when they actively participate in the learning programme; similarly, the best way to assess their progress is to involve them in the process. Participative assessment does not exclude formal testing methods, but asks the literacy worker to consider the learners as adults. If learners are to be encouraged to think about how they learn and their preferred way of learning, then it is important that assessment should follow this up. Learners can be encouraged to review their learning styles and see how effective they have been over time.

Real activities for teaching and learning are generally more meaningful for adults than text-book exercises. The same is true for assessment. Wherever possible, the assessment activity should be a real one, examining, for example, the way in which learners actually keep accounts; or how frequently and for what purposes they use the post office. There are many occasions when literacy skills can be demonstrated and assessed in learners' daily lives, rather than in exercises in the classroom.

Assessing literacy is a process of identifying, recognising, and describing progress and change. If we are concerned only with measuring progress, we tend to look only for evidence that can be quantified, such as statistics, grades, and percentages. If, however, we ask learners to describe their own progress, we get qualitative responses, such as *'I can now read the signs in the clinic'* or *'I read the lesson in church on Easter Sunday'*. If learning is assessed in both qualitative and quantitative ways, the information produced is more complete and more useful.

In Chapter 4, we suggested that assessment procedures should be discussed with all the relevant parties. The process of assessment provides excellent opportunities to encourage adult learners to take some responsibility for their own learning. This happens in a variety of ways.

- Discussing assessment with learners and involving them in the process will encourage them to be analytical about their own work and that of others. It will help them to understand why they are doing things and how the programme is intended to work.

- Assessment and evaluation activities involve learners in literacy and numeracy tasks, and offer real reasons for reading and writing. They can actually be used to promote literacy. For example, learners should be encouraged to keep written records of their work — a good reason for writing; and then, after some period of time, they will need to read their records in order to identify change and progress — a good reason for reading. Similarly, keeping attendance records offers real opportunities for working with numbers.

Assessing weaknesses as well as strengths

Recognising failure and difficulty is an important part of learning. Learners are often all too aware of their weaknesses, but are sometimes afraid of exposing them to scrutiny. Past experiences can block present progress. Some teachers punish children for their weaknesses! Glenys Kinnock, a British teacher and now a Member of the European Parliament, recalls a maths teacher from her childhood:

When she saw that I couldn't do it, she'd come over and slap the backs of my hands really hard. I was smacked and smacked, and the more she did it, the less likely it became that I'd ever be able to do any maths. She froze my brain.[16]

Sharing a problem

For some learners it is a great relief to be able to talk about a problem; they find that another learner or the literacy worker can help them work out ways of dealing with it. If assessment is promoted as a means of identifying both strengths and weaknesses, in order to provide support, then it should have a positive and encouraging outcome for the learner. Assessment in this formative context is about *supporting* learners, rather than merely judging them. Succeeding in assessments is a wonderful motivating tonic for learners. To see evidence of one's successes and achievements and to have others recognise them is a very strong motivator and gives great pleasure. Praise works wonders!

Methods of assessment

As with methods of teaching and learning, there is no single correct method for assessment. Whatever methods are chosen will reflect the ideas of those who plan the assessment. The decision is as much a political one as an educational one, and will need careful consideration. It is important to ensure that the methods of assessment reflect those that are being adopted for teaching and learning.

In the early days of literacy campaigns, formal test methods, including standardised tests of reading, comprehension, and spelling, were used to assess adult learners. These tests, designed and normed for children, were soon found to be unhelpful and inappropriate when used with adults. A person of 45, told that he or she has a reading age of 7, is most likely to feel foolish and inadequate. To examine adults on tests designed for children is a nonsense. Now, however, times are changing and a wider range of methods, formal and informal, quantitative and qualitative, is increasingly being recognised as valuable.

Assessment is a form of research, and, as in any research, it is good practice to use more than one method for collecting data. It is a good idea to choose two or three methods that complement each other, give variety, and will provide the most complete picture possible.

Monitor and record how the learners are progressing at regular intervals and note down times when either of you feels that a specific breakthrough has been made, or when there seems to be a blockage or difficulty.

There are some general approaches that are worth considering. We will look at four of them.

Group review/class meeting

The group review is one of the simplest and most effective ways of obtaining a wealth of information and encouraging learners to share their ideas, to analyse problems, and to think about their own learning styles. It can de-personalise difficulties and set the scene for individual interviews.

Here is a list of possible questions. They should be adapted according to the particular cultural and linguistic context of the group.

- Are you enjoying the programme?
- Are you benefiting as you expected to?
- Have you found it too slow? Too fast?
- What have you most enjoyed?
- What have you most disliked?
- What changes or additions would you like to suggest?
- Are there any questions you'd like to ask?
- Are you expected to do too much homework?
- Are the sessions too long? Too short?
- Some learners have left the programme. Do you have any idea why?

Large groups can be divided into smaller groups of three–five learners. It is sometimes helpful to leave the groups to work on their own. They can then come back together again to discuss conclusions and recommendations.

Individual interviews

Personal interviews are valuable all through (and beyond) the programme. Literacy workers usually interview each learner, but, alternatively, learners could interview each other in pairs and report the information orally, as pictures, or in written or tape-recorded form.

Learners must be comfortable and happy about being interviewed on their own. Some cultures and religions may object to individual interviews (for example, if a woman is interviewed by a man).

Even though interviews can follow a range of directions, it is useful to think out and write down questions in advance. Open-ended questions are better than closed questions which can be answered merely by 'yes' or 'no'. *What, why, how, where,* and *when* are useful words for beginning open-ended questions. 'What did you do in the class last week?' 'How is being able to read a little helping at home?' 'What have you needed to write recently?' 'What would you like to be able to read?' This is the time to refer to the records which learners and literacy workers have been keeping: they will be a useful source of information for discussion and comparison. Here are a few tips.

- Prepare for the interview: have a preliminary meeting with the learner and discuss what will happen in the interview, its purpose, and how you will each prepare for it.

- Make sure that you both feel comfortable. The setting can be very informal, but the meeting should be free from interruptions.

- Prepare the questions carefully.

- Don't start asking questions immediately. Talk generally until the learner relaxes a little.

- Be sensitive to the feelings of the individual.

- Be willing to spend more time; don't be in a hurry.

- Listen to what is being said. Ask questions to clarify your understanding. Show that you are listening, by repeating some of what the learner has said. Summarise what he or she has said, using your own words.

- Encourage the learner to ask questions too, and be prepared to answer them as fully as possible.

- Take only brief notes, or tape-record the session.

- Show your notes to the learner.

Observation of classes

Literacy workers often find it uncomfortable to have someone watching them teach, and will argue that it makes the lesson artificial. This barrier is worth overcoming. Observation is an extremely useful method of assessment and evaluation. All those involved — the observer, the literacy worker, and the learners — need to recognise that the purpose is *support*, not judgement. Before an observer comes into a session, there should be some discussion about what he or she is being asked to observe. Feedback is almost always useful to the literacy worker; observers are in a good position to notice how learners are responding and coping. The purpose is not to set a test, but to obtain accurate information about everyday practices which can later be discussed, leading to a better programme.

One can also learn much to impove one's own teaching from being an observer of other workers' classes.

Casual conversations and observations

It is worth the effort to be alert to information and impressions exchanged during tea-breaks, before and after class, and in other chance meetings with learners. Non-verbal behaviour, like gestures and facial expressions, can also be very revealing. Observations like these are rarely called methods, but they are likely to provide excellent information, which can be usefully followed up later.

The whole or the parts?

Literacy and numeracy involve reading, writing, listening, speaking, calculating, and having the confidence to *use* these skills at will. Often a literacy or numeracy task involves more than one skill; sometimes it can be assessed as a complete task, sometimes it is more appropriate to focus on just one skill, or a component of that skill.

Assessing reading

In the early stages of learning to read and write, it is sometimes easier to look at the parts that go to make up the whole. Each part can be split into even smaller parts — such as reading for speed, or fluency, or understanding — and progress in each can be assessed, if it is felt to be useful.

Checking on reading can be done in many different ways. Here are some ideas to get started.

- Talk with learners about their progress in reading. What are they coping with in class? What can they cope with outside the classroom? What words or phrases are they recognising in their local community, for example at the shop or the clinic?

- Reading aloud is often used for assessment, but we should remember that it is a very different activity from reading silently. Some readers may be shy about reading out loud to others. Few adults need to read to an audience in their everyday lives. But reading to groups of children (in school, or at home) provides a chance for adults to practise their reading skills. There might be an opportunity here for assessment. Learners could report on how they are doing, and the children might also offer their comments.

- Fluency in reading to others can be assessed by a simple but effective procedure known as *mis-cue analysis*. The learner reads aloud, while the assessor marks a copy of what is being read, noting mistakes, hesitations, and alterations to the text, which are then analysed and discussed. This is one way to assess fluency and to discover what strategies a reader is using for tackling a new word or deriving meaning from a text. But it is not a test of any other form of reading skill.

- It is possible to check fluency and speed in silent reading (or 'sub-vocalised' reading, in which readers say the words quietly to themselves), by checking how far the reader gets in a given time, or how long it takes him or her to read a passage. But it is important to check that they are also reading for understanding. We need to think about why we might decide to use this form of assessment — or decide against it. What will it achieve? What will it tell us? What will it tell the learner?

- Learners can be asked to set questions about a passage they have read. They will find this difficult if they have not understood the passage. This exercise could be done in pairs and tried out orally with other learners.

- Filling in the gaps (or *Cloze procedure*), as described in Chapter 7, can also be used to check on understanding. If the reader does not comprehend the passage, he or she will have difficulty in filling in the gaps in ways that make sense. When using this style of exercise, we should remember that a gap can often be filled by more than one word: for example, in the sentence *The sky was .... before the rain came*, the gap could be filled by a number of alternatives, such as *dark/angry/heavy/cloudy*. The main value of gap-filling exercises lies in talking with learners about why they responded as they did. This will provide insights into how they are approaching the reading task, and how it relates to their own experiences.

- Paired reading can be used for assessment purposes, by noting and observing the improvement which the learner is making over time.

- Real-life situations are more meaningful than text-book tests. Can the learner identify words in a different context — for example, words like DANGER or OPEN or CLINIC? Learners could be asked to report other uses of such words outside the classroom. Finding a familiar word used in a new context gives learners a real sense of satisfaction. Such instances should be recorded and, where possible, learners should be encouraged to record their own observations.

- Learners' Reading Diets can be analysed. This involves the learner and the literacy worker in keeping a note of all the learner's reading activities during a particular period. It could be done for a week early on in the programme and then a further week some time later, and at regular intervals. Is the list expanding? What is on it? Why isn't it changing? Are there things the learner would like to read, but doesn't have access to? Keep a note of the discussion and the learner's feelings.

- Marking or proof-reading someone else's work can provide an opportunity for assessing reading skills. How easily and how accurately do learners manage the task? Can they identify mistakes? Can they correct them?

- Have they been able to read something which they couldn't have coped with previously? What have they read? What did they feel about it?

- Do they dare to try reading something now that they would have avoided before?

- Ask learners to read a passage and answer questions. The questions and responses can be given orally. If they are new readers, writing answers may be beyond their skills, and we should remember that we are assessing reading, not writing, in this instance. If we discuss learners' answers with them straight away, we may find out more about how they are working and thinking.

- Can they read a map, find the railway lines, point to the north/south/east/west, etc.?

The passage for testing comprehension should be chosen carefully, considering whether it is too easy or too difficult for the learners. Difficulty depends not only on the complexity of language and style in which it is written, and on its lay-out and print style, but also on the reader's experience.

Setting questions needs planning, too: how they are phrased and how they are ordered affect how difficult they are. We should make sure that the reading and writing levels required of learners are commensurate with their skills. If test questions are written in a form that is beyond the skill of the readers, then they won't be able to answer the question, although they may know the answer.

Assessing writing

- Keeping examples of learners' writing offers an easy way of measuring progress. Has there been an improvement over time? It is useful to collect bits and pieces of writing in a folder. In this way, learners can begin to build up a portfolio of their work. These will enable a comparison between what it was like a few weeks or months ago and what it is like now. Without the early examples to refer to, it is unlikely that either the learner or the literacy worker will remember what it was really like in the beginning. The learner can sort out the folder once in a while, using the opportunity for self-assessment.

- When assessing writing, it is important to be clear what particular aspects are being considered. Is it the handwriting, the ideas, the spelling, or grammar? Formal or informal styles?

- Learners' Writing Diets can be discussed, individually and as a group. They can be kept in the folder or portfolio. These 'diets' will provide the literacy worker with ideas for materials and lessons too.

- Learners could be asked to bring in a copy of something they have written at home.

- Learners could be asked how they feel about different aspects of writing and different sorts of writing. How confident are they now? What kind of writing do they most enjoy? Why? What do they find most difficult? Why? Exploring such questions will encourage the learners to think about how they work and will give the literacy worker an insight into their strengths and weaknesses, providing clues for future work.

- What were their aims as regards writing? Have these been met? If not, why not? Have their aims changed? Keeping a record of aims and noting how they might have changed over time provides evidence of progress.

- How much help do they need now in correcting their own work? How does this compare with earlier efforts?

- Very often, fellow learners will have noted how someone's confidence is improving. A comment like 'You wouldn't have tried that a month ago' can do wonders to boost morale. Encourage discussion about progress and achievements.

Assessing spelling

- Spelling is usually best assessed in the context of a piece of writing. Spelling words in isolation is only part of the process of enabling learners to use them whenever they are needed. But it can occasionally be useful to give a list of spellings to be learned, if only to boost confidence. The list should be created from the vocabulary that the learners are using, and the learners could help to create the test, by identifying words with which they have difficulty. But the list should also include some that they are certain to get right. It is a good idea to teach them to spell a long word and then put it in the test. Long words are often easier to get right than short words which are similar to other words — but it feels good to get a long word right. Words that are similar should not be put close together in a test. The words being tested should be used in a sentence rather than in isolation.

- Proof-reading is another way to assess spelling. Learners can mark their own work, starting by putting a mark next to any word that they think is wrong. If they can, they should correct the errors themselves. Can they suggest what to change in order to correct the spelling? If they can identify that something is wrong, even if they cannot correct it, they are part-way to correcting or proof-reading their work. They may need to be assured that recognising errors and having an idea about how to correct them, or being able to make the correction themselves, indicates learning and progress. The exercise should be treated as proof-reading, rather than a test. It can also be done as a group exercise, if handled sensitively.

- There are 'good' or 'positive' mistakes and 'poor' or 'negative' mistakes. 'Good' mistakes are those which enable the reader to recognise the intended word. If the mistake is a logical one (if the writer's strategy can be identified), then it is a 'good' mistake. For example, the learner may write, 'Miriam was asked to reed a book.' It is clear from the rest of the sentence that 'reed' should be 'read'. That the writer used 'ee' is understandable: 'ee' can represent the same sound as 'ea'. A 'good' mistake can be used to illustrate improvement; helping learners to identify why it is wrong will help them to get it right next time.

  'Negative' mistakes are those where it is difficult to see any strategy, and the correct word cannot be worked out. These are more difficult to correct and will need special attention. The learner should be asked why he or she has spelt the word that way. Finding out what strategies a learner adopts will help the literacy worker to think of ways to help them.

Assessing numeracy

Many of the strategies for assessing reading, writing, and spelling described above can be used for numeracy too. Try to be aware at all times of the numeracy activities in which learners are engaged, at home and in the community. Collect examples of daily tasks that involve numeracy and observe how the learners tackle them. Ensure that the levels of difficulty are not beyond them. (This applies to the numeracy element, and may also apply to the reading and writing involved.) Here are some other strategies which you may find useful.

- Play number games and have quizzes.
- Observe learners working on their own and in pairs or small groups. Who does what?
- Ask the learners to devise questions for each other. Let them mark their own work and each other's work.

- Talk about difficulties as a group.
- Hold individual interviews with learners.
- Is their speed improving?
- Is accuracy improving?
- Can they identify areas of numeracy where they have difficulty?
- Can learners help or teach each other?
- Can they do the calculation orally?
- Are they daring to try tasks more readily than they were?
- Short informal tests, given in a friendly setting, could be organised. You could use a variety of tools, such as a box of matches, a basket of fruit, or a roll of sweets, to check learners' progress in addition, subtraction, and division.

Progress profiles

Figure 9.1 (overleaf) shows part of a progress review sheet, taken from *The Progress Profile*, an assessment approach which was developed for ALBSU (the Adult Literacy Basic Skills Unit in the UK).[17]

The Progress Profile enables a learner and a literacy worker to record the learner's aims, break them down into smaller parts, and return to them after a period of time and discuss progress. Sometimes learners' aims alter over time, or parts of the original aim become irrelevant. The original aims should not be forgotten, but it may be necessary to review them regularly. Looking at the differences between the learner's original aims and current aims will provide useful evidence of progress. It is rather like noting how a child has grown: unless someone previously marked the child's height on the wall, it is hard to know how much he or she has grown.

Standards

Not all literacy and numeracy tasks need to be done perfectly or meet formal standards. Shopping lists and other notes that we write for ourselves need not be written very neatly or spelt flawlessly. If it works as a reminder for the person who wrote it, it is doing its job. Often we don't need to know exactly how much our shopping bill adds up to, but we may want to estimate the cost, to make sure we have enough money to pay for it. Rounding up and rounding down the actual prices may give us a close enough figure.

Similarly, not all reading tasks require 100 per cent comprehension. For example, a reader may glance through a newspaper quickly, to pick up on the main headlines (skim reading) or look for a particular piece of information in a book (scanning), such as the name of a particular fertiliser or where the nearest health clinic is. In such instances it is not necessary to read and understand the rest of the text. However, there will be times when it is crucial to comprehend all of the information

PROGRESS REVIEW

READING · WRITING · LISTENING · SPEAKING · CONFIDENCE

Aims	Elements	
To read Samuel's letters	To practise reading his writing	To practise reading other letters and notes
Look at the Elements and shade in the amount you have achieved ▲		To learn to spell his name and address so that I can write back
To write a note for my mother that she can read	To spell my mother's name and address	To practise my writing so that it will look neat
Look at the Elements and shade in the amount you have achieved ▲		To find my spelling mistakes for myself
I want to add up what I must pay at the shop	To add up the different things I want to buy	To check if I have enough money to pay for them
Look at the Elements and shade in the amount you have achieved ▲		To check if the shop gives me the right money back (change)

How have you used what you have learned?

I can read my son's letter on my own.
I wrote a note to my mother.
I checked my money at the shop — I was right.

(reading in depth), such as reading instructions for mixing up feed for a baby. Mathematical accuracy may be critical, for example in measuring a patient's medication or in sowing seed.

Literacy workers should be careful not to assess tasks beyond the levels of understanding, accuracy, and presentation that are required in their real application in everyday life. This is pointless. A good test is to apply the 'ABC' technique:

A is for Accurate
B is for Brief
C is for Clear.

Of any piece of work, we can ask *How accurate is it? How brief is it? How clear is it?* But we should also ask: *How accurate/brief/clear does it need to be?* The assessment should be clearly related to the purpose of the task. We are trying to help learners to function more effectively in their daily lives. This is known as the 'good enough' principle. If we are clear about the purpose of the task, we will be able to identify the standards required.

This realistic attitude will encourage learners to try their learning in situations outside the classroom, to talk through their successes and failures with the literacy worker, and to have realistic expectations of themselves. Helping them to use their literacy and numeracy independently and in collaboration with others is what we should be aiming for.

Assessing teaching

Like learners, literacy workers value the comments of others — and take more kindly to positive feedback than to negative criticism. Feedback is likely to come unexpectedly and sometimes from unusual places.

The following checklist is designed to help literacy workers to monitor their own teaching: to identify their own strengths and weaknesses, as well as those of the funding or providing organisation. It might be productive for a group of colleagues to go through the list together. (It is not intended to be complete: feel free to add to it.)

Learning environment
- How suitable and comfortable is the place where I teach?
- Is there enough light?
- Is it warm enough or cool enough?
- Is it clean?
- Can it be made more welcoming?
- What aids are available (a board, pencils, paper, a collection of reading material, etc.)?

Class/group management
- Do I always address the whole group when I am teaching?
- Can I create variety by asking them to work in pairs, and in smaller groups?

117

- How can different groups be given different parts of a task?
- How can one person help another?

Presentation, development, organisation
- How well do I present new ideas to learners?
- Do the learners and I have a clear idea of what we are trying to achieve, and how we might get there?
- Do we go back over what we did the week before?
- How do I help learners to build on what we have already done?

Motivating learners
- How do I try to motivate the learners?
- How do I praise their work?
- How do I encourage them?
- Do I help them when they need it?
- Do they ask for help?
- Do I recognise the times when they need support?

Attention to individuals
- Does everyone in the group receive attention from me?
- Do I give much more attention to some people than others?
- Does anyone feel left out?

Assessment and record keeping
- What records do I keep?
- What use are they to me?
- Do I involve the learners in keeping records?
- How could we work on this together?
- How do we use the records (monitoring and planning; assessment and evaluation)?

Teaching aids and materials
- What teaching aids do I use?
- Can I create some variety by using some different resources?
- Can I or the learners make some teaching aids or materials?
- How are the learners involved in developing materials?

Variety of teaching methods
- Do I always teach the same topic in the same way?
- What other methods could I use?

lectures	group work
drama	role play
discussion	making materials
worksheets	creating a newsletter
brainstorming	visits
problem-solving	inviting a colleague to teach with me
etc.	etc.

Involving the learners

- How much do I involve the learners in
- identifying their needs
- planning how we will meet those needs
- choosing and developing materials
- keeping records
- assessing their own work
- assessing my teaching?

Literacy workers should also ask themselves if they are enjoying the experience, and what kind of support they would like. Remember that it is not always necessary to have sophisticated, expensive equipment. If the literacy worker and the learners are enthusiastic, if they respect each other and agree on their aims, they are well on the way to success.

Assessing learning and teaching should help the literacy worker and the learners to identify what has been achieved, to plan confidently for the next phase, and to build stronger relationships, so that they can all enjoy the learning experience still more.

Evaluating impact: literacy in action

Impact evaluation is concerned with the effects of learning and the programme on participants' lives and those of their communities. Some of these outcomes may be anticipated, some not. The following examples, quoted from VSO and Oxfam reports, provide an insight into the benefits that learning literacy can bring to people's lives. The outcomes may sometimes be unexpected, but are valuable and worth recording.

... As we spoke in the yard of the Centre, someone called over the fence to give Miriam a letter that had just arrived from her daughter. She opened it and beamed. 'Now I am very happy, because I can read it on my own.' ...

... The impact of the CNTC programme on the co-operative has been substantial. The co-op meetings are now attended by almost all members, whereas in the past an attendance of half was considered good. Those who do not turn up usually send written apologies. People arrive punctually and work through a clear agenda ...

... Now most of us in the Co-op can read and write, so we can do things that were unimaginable before ...

... The level of participation in discussions has increased beyond recognition. If someone thinks something, they know when and how to say it. In the past we were mostly silent ...

Impact evaluation is concerned with evaluating what is happening in the everyday world of the learners. The evaluation situations are not contrived, unlike classroom exercises. Evaluating the impact of a programme is the clearest way of identifying its successes and failures. The programme has been successful if the participants are using their learning to do things in their lives more easily and more confidently than they did before; or if the experience has motivated them to 'have a go' or risk trying to do something new or in a different way. If, however, learners feel discouraged and are reluctant to use their improved literacy skills in their lives outside the classroom, then development workers, organisers, funders, and learners themselves may have reason to be disappointed or to feel that something is lacking in the programme.

Measures of success

Using literacy and numeracy in daily life

One way to measure success is to ask how the learners apply their new or improved literacy and numeracy skills in their daily lives.

- Do they read instructions, or try to read them?
- Are they confident enough to write a note or letter?
- Will they risk making some mistakes in a piece of writing?
- Can they work out costs?
- Do they do appropriate calculations?
- Do they check the calculations of others and dare to challenge them?
- Do they still require as much help to read and write as they did at the start of the programme?

Being able to spell words in a classroom test is one thing, but getting them correct in a piece of writing that someone else is going to read is a different matter. Knowing which arithmetical procedures to apply to solve a problem in the workplace shows that the person has real understanding and is confident to apply his or her knowledge.

Confidence

The key aim of all literacy programmes is to enable learners to use literacy to benefit their lives. This means that, besides learning the skills of reading, writing, listening, speaking, and numeracy, they also need to gain enough confidence to put these skills into practice in any situation they want to. Many programmes aim to help learners to become independent and not require anyone else's help in carrying out a literacy or numeracy task. Will they have the confidence and independence to check the shopkeeper's addition in front of him, or write a letter without asking anyone to check the spelling? Using literacy skills in real situations is the aim of the programme, and therefore it should be the aim of evaluation to check whether or not it is happening, and to what extent.

To evaluate the effects of the programme outside the classroom is to evaluate at a level that is different from testing skills within the classroom. The two approaches should complement each other; they explore slightly different things. Classroom assessments can help to boost confidence and motivate the learners to persevere and practise. Getting feedback from impact evaluation outside the classroom can expand the learners' ideas about their skills and confidence. The process can lead to wider applications and sustained learning; for example, reading a letter successfully may lead to reading other materials, or writing a reply, and so on.

Literacy for living

Literacy programmes often refer to 'literacy for independence', apparently implying that an individual should be able to perform all literacy and numeracy tasks alone and unaided. While such independence is important, we need also to recognise that many literacy tasks are achieved with the support of other people. Perhaps programmes should refer also to 'literacy for interdependence', and perhaps this aspect of literacy should be assessed and evaluated. Having the confidence to work with other people is not to be dismissed lightly, and may be a significant measure of learners' progress and achievement. Collecting information of this nature will help to provide a truer picture of the impact of the literacy programme.

Think about a piece of writing, such as a report, that you have recently produced. Did you talk over the ideas or format with someone? Did you ask a friend or colleague to read it through or check it? Many literacy tasks involve more than one person, and we all involve others in literacy and numeracy tasks when we think it would be helpful. When did you last ask someone how to spell a word or check a calculation, rather than use a dictionary or re-do the calculation yourself?

Impact evaluation is about identifying literacy in action. Evaluation methods should therefore allow for the collaborative nature of many literacy tasks, collecting information and recording how learners work with other people, as well as how they cope independently.

Motivation

Evaluation is a means to an end, as well as being an end in itself. It is a way of demonstrating to the learners that they do have the confidence to use their literacy, that they can dare to try things. It is a means of empowering learners. Recognising that they have tried and achieved things that they would not have done previously boosts morale and self-esteem. Most of us, not just learners, need someone else to notice our achievements. Self-evaluation is a skill that is often not very well developed and needs to be encouraged. However, feedback from literacy workers, fellow learners, family members, and the wider community can be supportive and instructive, providing great encouragement and motivation.

Sustainability

Literacy and numeracy skills need to be *used* if they are to be maintained and further developed. Research shows that, unless the skills are practised, they are mostly lost. All the hard work of the learners and the development workers is in danger of being wasted, if the learning does not become part of the learners' lives. Literacy is best acquired by using it, and therefore data should be collected to show how this is happening, and this information should be used to support learning. Monitoring, or keeping diets of reading, writing, and numeracy, will also help to establish the practice of using literacy and numeracy at home, at work, and in community life, while simultaneously avoiding the loss of skills and promoting further development.

Who will evaluate?

The evaluation may involve independent individuals from outside the programme. Local health workers or agricultural extension staff may be encouraged to review how the literacy programme is contributing to their training and other programmes. Common aims may be agreed and complementary approaches sought. Funders often insist on such external evaluation.

Evaluation should take evidence from all categories of participants: learners, development workers, planners, and the wider community. The primary aim of such internal evaluation may be to improve future practice, learn from mistakes, and contribute to strategic planning. Some training may be necessary for potential evaluators. It could include sessions on giving and receiving feedback; observation techniques; questioning techniques; agreeing an observation checklist; and keeping records.

Self-evaluation is also to be encouraged. Learners need to develop the confidence to rely on their own judgements, rather than always depending on other people; but this is not an easy task! Most of us have always experienced evaluation as something which other people did to us: the examiner was all-important and all-powerful.

Establishing trust

Learning how to evaluate one's own progress and to trust one's own judgement are important aspects of empowerment. They should be part of a participatory curriculum. Since what we are trying to establish in a participatory approach to learning is open communication and the confidence to take risks, there needs to be a degree of trust between learner and literacy worker. Similarly, to evaluate how learning is affecting behaviour and attitudes outside the classroom requires openness and trust. These ways of assessing and evaluating may be quite new for the learners. They may be new for literacy workers too, and will need careful introduction and discussion.

As trust grows, motivation and responsibility increase, and the gap between literacy worker and learner closes. A partnership is created. If we want to be trusted, we must be honest and sincere; we must respect learners' confidences; we must keep our agreements; we should always communicate directly, and resist the temptation to try to manipulate others.

How to evaluate?

Impact evaluation is frequently done informally, and is often based on the anecdotes and observations reported by learners, development workers, and others. Comments by the elders in a community can provide evidence of progress and achievement. For example:

In discussion with a group of learners in a fishing village on the outskirts of Madras, the interviewer noticed an old lady sitting quietly by. With a little encouragement, she talked of her observations and how the confidence and attitudes of the women had changed as a result of attending the literacy classes. They now challenged the men about various issues. They made demands for their children. They insisted on continuing with the classes. The women were surprised. They had not noticed the changes themselves.[18]

Evidence like this is worth considering, but we cannot rely on such informal methods alone. We need to create a more structured approach, based on methods that are appropriate, including the following:

- observation
- interviews
- keeping diaries
- keeping portfolios
- comparing reading and writing diets — then and now
- class review meetings.

All these approaches are considered in some detail in the section on Assessment earlier in this chapter.

Clearly the methods and indicators chosen must be relevant to the particular programme. Contexts will determine what is appropriate, but it is often helpful to have some ideas to start with. Here are some indicators of progress, suggested during a recent workshop in Bangladesh.[19]

- Increases in the level of income.
- Degree of record keeping by groups/learners (such as handling group accounts or taking minutes).
- Levels of participation in community organisations.
- Knowledge of key health issues and how to do certain productive activities.
- Impact on children's education (attendance and achievement at school).

- Impact on gender relations/household decision-making.
- Mobility from the home.
- Attitudes to the local languages.
- Levels of self-confidence (e.g. people's willingness to speak in meetings).
- Analytical abilities (answers to questions like: *why do prices change?*).
- Case studies of literacy learners (randomly selected, semi-structured interviews).
- Case-studies of classes/villages (including interviews with other members of the community).
- Case-studies of facilitators (literacy workers), to determine the impact on their own lives and any emergence as role models/community activists.

Conclusion

Assessment and evaluation are genuinely integral to learning and teaching. They can help learners and development workers to understand what they are doing and why, and to work collaboratively towards making the whole experience more relevant and worthwhile. The practices of collecting information, keeping records, monitoring progress, analysing, and discussing are all ways of encouraging learners to use their literacy skills, at the same time as helping them to become more responsible adult learners, capable and confident of playing their role in the wider community. There are no losers: everyone wins. The skills needed for impact evaluation are skills of observation and reflection. They are not new, but they will need to be practised — by learners, literacy workers, and all the other evaluators. Evaluation does happen informally all the time, but it will be more effective if we structure it and consciously improve our skills.

PART FOUR

Materials for Literacy

Katmandu, Nepal: materials for literacy!
Photo: Omar Sattaur

CHAPTER 10

'Special' materials

Choosing literacy materials

When people are learning to read and write, they clearly need something to read and something to write about. The lack of appropriate and available materials is often felt to be a problem in literacy classes.

Many literacy programmes are based on a primer: a highly structured workbook which introduces learners to a new lesson and a new topic, often a new letter, on every page. Many primers contain 'write-on' pages, on which the learner is asked to copy letters or words. Others form the first of a series of carefully graded readers and give comparatively little attention to writing at all. In most cases, the resources that literacy workers feel they lack are these artificially created materials for reading and/or writing. We considered the advantages and disadvantages of using primers in Chapter 5. A large number of literacy programmes continue to use these or other specially prepared materials, but they are rarely the only printed matter available, and they may not be the most useful.

No approach to teaching literacy is neutral. While some materials are essential, learning literacy skills and learning literacy practices go hand in hand. *People who are taught to read a primer learn to read a primer, and may not learn to read other more useful material.* The skills involved in reading a primer are not automatically transferable. People who are taught to decipher and to use ordinary, everyday materials, or those materials which are valuable to their everyday lives, are more likely to develop real literacy practices, as well as skills. Before assuming that a literacy programme needs specially written materials, it might be useful to take an overview of the range of printed or written matter that is available in the area where classes are taking place.

This chapter will give a brief description of specially produced literacy materials and consider the advantages and the problems concerned with using them.

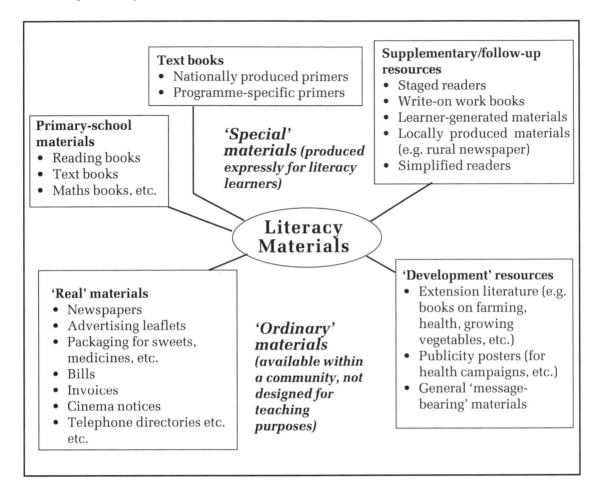

Text books
- Nationally produced primers
- Programme-specific primers

Supplementary/follow-up resources
- Staged readers
- Write-on work books
- Learner-generated materials
- Locally produced materials (e.g. rural newspaper)
- Simplified readers

Primary-school materials
- Reading books
- Text books
- Maths books, etc.

'Special' materials (produced expressly for literacy learners)

Literacy Materials

'Real' materials
- Newspapers
- Advertising leaflets
- Packaging for sweets, medicines, etc.
- Bills
- Invoices
- Cinema notices
- Telephone directories etc. etc.

'Ordinary' materials (available within a community, not designed for teaching purposes)

'Development' resources
- Extension literature (e.g. books on farming, health, growing vegetables, etc.)
- Publicity posters (for health campaigns, etc.)
- General 'message-bearing' materials

Figure 10.1: Literacy materials: 'special' and 'ordinary'

(Adapted from Rogers 1994)

Ready-made structured courses

Adult literacy activities are sometimes based on the primary-school approach of progressing from a simple primer through a series of graded and carefully structured stages. An elaborate scheme gradually introduces new words and increasingly complex sentences. The scheme may be based on the number of letters in a word, the number of words on a page, or the frequency with which one word appears. This is an approach favoured by UNESCO in particular. PROAP (Principal Regional Office for Asia and the Pacific) has developed a table, setting out standard word counts and writing skills for each different level and ability. For example:

Reading Skills: Post-Literacy Level 1
Words: Small known words
Sentence length: 8 words
Paragraph length: 80 words

Total words: 500 — 1,000
Number of pages: 16 — 20

Writing Skills
Format: Personal letter
Simple story
Personal biography

The PROAP primers and workbooks are produced regionally, and written by literacy workers during workshops which involve represent-atives from a number of countries. The workers meet together, discuss the particular problems in their areas, decide on themes for readers, and write the texts themselves. These are briefly field-tested (given to groups of learners to read and comment on) and then taken back to each member country to be translated into the languages used in the literacy classes.

Most schemes contain more reading materials than writing materials. The writing materials that do exist are often in the form of 'write-on' workbooks, which give examples of letters (sometimes with arrows indicating pen direction, or dots to be joined up) and words and sentences, with lines ruled on which to copy them.

Some workbooks give problems to be solved, such as gap-fill exercises, maths problems, sequencing activities using numbers and letters, and 'spot the difference' exercises. Books like this encourage people to *do* something with what they read, and aim to develop a more active and critical approach to written texts. But it is important not to make assumptions about what people will and will not understand. The rationale and the value of some of these types of exercise may need to be explained, and some may be based on cultural practices and conventions which are unfamiliar or irrelevant to the people using them.

Among literacy workers there is a continuing debate about the value of simplified readers. These are generally familiar or classical stories which have been re-written, using a simple vocabulary and sentences, paragraphs, and pages of predetermined lengths. However, there is no real evidence to prove that word-length is significant when learning to read. While it is true that over-complicated texts and long sentences present problems, learners do use quite an elaborate written vocabulary if it is relevant to them. People will tackle material they are interested in and texts they can identify with, regardless of the length of the words. The lay-out and the organisation of text is generally a more significant factor. Newspaper headlines, for example, are easier to read than the printed text underneath. It may be preferable to help learners to develop strategies for understanding the things they want to read, rather than choosing books for them and artificially simplifying the texts.

An alternative approach could be to cut and rearrange material chosen by learners and put it into a more manageable form. Some guidelines for the organisation of materials are suggested below.

Locally produced materials

Literacy workers may wish to use the structured materials produced by organisations like UNESCO. However, they should also ask themselves if they might serve local needs better by developing local materials. Ready-made texts may not serve the needs of the learners. The subjects they discuss and the particular literacy practices they teach are decided in advance and by outsiders. Moreover, materials created on a large scale and outside the programme are often written or designed by someone whose cultural background is different from that of the learners. Even where materials are created locally, however, the writer or artist is in danger of making assumptions about what the learners need and what conventions they will understand.

Another disadvantage of specially produced materials is that they are often cheaply produced, of poor quality, and reproduced so many times on copiers and stencils that in the end they are scarcely legible.

Learners and literacy workers may become over-dependent on books and primers, which can be mislaid or fail to arrive. These somewhat artificial materials are often produced by small organisations with limited funds, who then have difficulty in supplying them to the users. Much time and money may be invested in trying to produce relevant materials, but if they fail to appear regularly, learners may become reluctant to continue learning.

Practical guidelines for producing literacy materials[20]

If, after considering all the pitfalls we have described, you decide to produce your own materials, here are some guidelines which may help to avoid some of the problems.

Books and booklets
- Print the covers, if possible, and use bright background colours.
- Use clear, bold type on the front cover.
- Centre the title on the cover.
- Print text in solid black on a clean background, to give as much contrast as possible.
- Use a durable cover, as stiff as possible.
- For the text, use paper dense enough to prevent the ink showing through from the reverse side.
- If stapling, use strong, tightly closed brass staples, and use tape on the inside of the spine.
- If binding, choose glue that will not go brittle in high temperatures.
- Trim the edges of the cover after binding; overlapping covers are not a good idea, as the corners will become damaged or torn.

Text letter-forms
- Use a type that is clear and open. With a Roman alphabet, select a

suitable typeface, taking care to avoid one that confuses letter forms or symbols; for example, the letter **l** and and the number **1** look very similar in some type-faces.

- Aim for clarity and consistency, with characters large enough for everyone to see them clearly.
- Start off with larger type sizes, and gradually progress to smaller letter sizes.
- As a minimum, the lower-case x should be at least 2 mm high, and the upper-case X at least 3 mm high; you risk straining people's eyes if you choose a smaller size.

Letters for copying
- Use letters that are clear and simple.
- Present only a few words at a time.
- Leave comfortable spaces between the letters and between the lines. (Remember that handwriting uses a lot of space.)
- Start with letters at least 2 cm high.

Margins
- Margins are always necessary: they make a text easier to handle and to read.
- Keep them consistent throughout a piece of writing.
- Make them large enough for the hand to hold the page without covering the text.
- But don't make them too big: too much space will suggest material that is intended for children.

Text and images
- Where pictures and words appear together, they should support each other. Make sure that the relationship between the text and the image is clear.
- Pictures need the same margins as text.
- It is generally better to put text above or underneath an image, rather than alongside it.

Page numbers
- It is helpful to number pages, even if a page contains only pictures — especially if the pictures are specially placed in relation to the text.
- Put the numbers in the same place on each page, and in a place where they can easily be seen.

Learner-generated materials

Learner-generated materials are written by learners for other learners to read, discuss, or learn from. The Language Experience Approach (described in Chapter 5) develops a lot of written text which can be used more extensively, either by the writer of the material, or by other learners, or within other programmes. Although most learner-generated material is used locally, there have been projects which circulate stories written by learners nationally and internationally, like the 'Round Robin' book which was sent to a number of literacy programmes around the world; each group of learners spent time reading the contributions of others in other programmes, before adding their own.

Community newspapers

One of the most common forms of locally produced, learner-generated materials is the community newspaper. Such materials are generally produced using low-cost, locally available printing methods, such as silk screen or stencil, and are written and illustrated by learners and literacy workers. They generally contain stories and articles about locally relevant issues, and are circulated through literacy programmes or sold in villages and through market places and bookstalls.

Although newspapers of this sort become more widely used when people have learned the basics of literacy (and are therefore able to make their own contribution), a skilled or inventive literacy worker may find ways of using them for initial literacy. Some can be produced as wall posters to be displayed within a classroom.

Producing a rural newspaper has many advantages:

- Readers arc involved in the writing and production of it, and in a real sense 'own' it.
- The writing and production of a community newspaper are a learning process which can increase learners' confidence.
- The publication is topical and current and produced at regular intervals (generally monthly or bi-monthly).
- It is concerned with things which readers may already know about, and people and places which they can identify with.
- It sets up a dialogue between people in neighbouring areas.
- It encourages the habit of reading newspapers as a source of information.

Rural newspaper projects can also present problems:

- They are rarely sustainable, and usually need external funding.
- Problems with reproduction and dissemination may make it hard to read or hard to get hold of.
- In a multilingual context, the choice of language is a difficult one, and the paper may need to print articles in different languages, or the same articles in translation. The use of translated text is never ideal.

The Atlantic Coast of Nicaragua is home to six different ethnic groups, each with its own language and distinctive way of life. In the late 1980s, the Sandinista government in Managua recognised the coastal peoples' right to develop their own cultural identities, and to administer their local affairs according to their traditions.

A community newspaper called *Sunrise* was developed with the help of Oxfam. Published monthly in English and Spanish (the two most widely used languages), *Sunrise* offered its readers a rich mixture of contents: baseball scores and obituaries, recipes and interviews, interspersed with articles about health and local history.

The newspaper was written and produced by a team of young school-leavers, using typesetting equipment supplied by Oxfam. Local people held raffles and reggae parties to raise the money to print the paper in Managua. The government paid the wages of the editorial team, but *Sunrise* never shrank from criticising the authorities. A favourite target was INE, the Nicaraguan Institute of Energy (known as 'INE-fficient' by local people); power cuts and inflated prices once prompted *Sunrise* to suggest that '*INE should donate some of their profits to the maternity ward at the hospital: we've had so many romantic dark nights lately that it will soon need to be expanded.*'

Copies of the newspaper always sold out within days. A member of the editorial team observed: '*At school we only studied the history of the Pacific Coast. Now we are discovering our own history. ... For the first time, Atlantic Coast people have seen themselves in photographs, and seen their own opinions recorded and taken seriously.*'

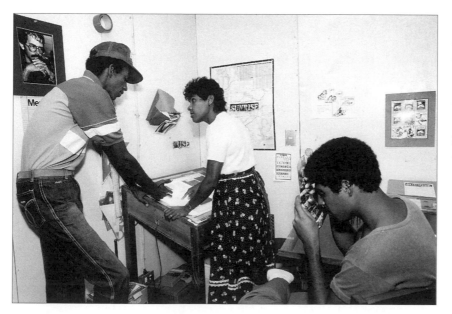

Bluefields, on the Atlantic Coast of Nicaragua: the office of 'Sunrise', a bilingual community newspaper, produced by a team of young people.
Photo: Mike Goldwater

133

Comic books

Comics are increasingly popular as a resource for literacy. In some areas of the world they are specially prepared for new readers. People who live in urban areas, where they are in contact with advertising materials and television, usually have few problems in interpreting the use of pictures and word bubbles in telling stories. Some comic books use photographs, which may be more easily recognised than line drawings.

However, in rural areas, where cartoon images or comic-book conventions are less familiar, the lay-out of a comic book may seem over-complicated. Some people will not have the visual literacy skills to interpret the images, or understand the direction or sequence in which to read. Comic books take a long time to produce and are seldom made for a very localised market. They need to be tested out with new readers and introduced gradually.

All locally produced materials need to be field-tested with learners at every stage. Never make assumptions about what people will be able to recognise or understand, or what they will want to do. Materials containing images or ideas which people can recognise and relate to are almost always easier to read.

In South Africa a group called 'Storyteller' produces comic books for young black readers. They are written in workshops, where young people from townships are introduced to a general theme and asked to act out a story around it. The dialogue is recorded, using as far as possible the language in which it is acted out; that is, the spoken language of the people who will read it. Anecdotes or jokes told during the workshop are also included, as are references to popular music or fashionable ideas. The stories are converted into comic books, using local artists who base their images on scenes from real life. Word bubbles contain the spoken language of the street, while the short written text that accompanies each image uses more formal English. Some of the strength and the value of Storyteller's work is in the time taken to reproduce not only language that people will identify with, but scenes and topics they will recognise. There is also a policy of trying to include ideas and opinions from all sections of the population, and therefore not stressing any one political or social line.

Academic resources

Primary-school materials

The problems involved in using primary-school materials with adult students can be anticipated. Although as initial materials they often deal with the basics of literacy or numeracy, they will have been written and

produced with children in mind. The examples and exercises used will reflect the interests of children, rather than the tasks which adults have to undertake, and in some cases the primary-school books available are imported from outside the local culture.

Some adults will be proud to be going to school and expect to work through the material that their children are using; others may find it offensive. Particularly in situations where learners have already been through the school system, having to use school books again may feel like an insult. Primary-school books are never very satisfactory, both in the tone they adopt towards learners and in the tasks they introduce.

However, they may be useful to literacy workers as a source book of examples, to be adapted for use with adult learners. What they do offer is a way of breaking down initial literacy skills into different tasks, and they present alternative ways of looking at the process of reading and writing.

The following exercise is from a child's maths book.

Alice and Peter are going on a picnic. They have four packets of crisps, eight sandwiches, two oranges, two round cakes, four apples, and one bottle of orange. They are each taking a friend with them on the picnic. How many children will there be altogether? Can you work out how much food each child will have? Can you write a sum for each different thing you have to work out?

This example, as well as being written for children, is clearly biased towards one particular culture. It is also based on a fictitious situation. Many cultures would be unfamiliar with the types of food described and also with this approach to dividing food among people. However, it can be adapted, as in the following exercise.

- How do you decide how much food you will need for a wedding feast?
- How do you work out how much it will cost?
- If you planned a wedding feast, how many people would you invite?
- What food would you need to buy?
- Try adding up the numbers of people.
- How many *chapatis* (or bread loaves, or rice, or maize) does each person generally eat?
- How many/how much would you need altogether?
- How many people can you feed from one sack of rice?
- Would two sacks of rice be enough for everyone?
- What are the advantages of being able to write all this down and calculate it?

A primary-school geography book often contains maps; a history book contains facts and information. While the maps may not reflect the locality in detail, nor the historical information relate directly to the learners, they may both give useful background information and suggest ways of presenting or phrasing exercises. It is important not to duplicate the childish examples or to oversimplify the situation, but a literacy worker with limited material can adapt and invent, using school books as a starting point.

Here are some questions to bear in mind.

- Is the exercise useful to these learners in this place?
- Does the exercise reflect the tasks they have to undertake in real life?
- Do any images reproduced relate to the situation in real life?
- Will these learners be able to identify with them?
- Is the information clear and comprehensible?
- Does it address the learners respectfully and as equals?
- Will anyone be embarrassed by this material?
- Is there an opportunity for learners to comment on and to challenge work that is presented for them to do?

Play, experimentation, and trying things out for oneself are very positive ways for adults as well as children to learn. If tasks are presented in an adult context, or in a way that is culturally acceptable, there is a lot to be gained from using simple examples. Be aware of the mood of the class, and adapt things accordingly!

Secondary-school materials

While secondary-school materials are designed for older children and are less simplistic in their approach, they generally reflect the subject-based approach of the school system. By this stage, formal education in a large number of countries has moved away from the creative, participative approach and is more concerned with presenting facts and teaching a body of knowledge.

For this reason, secondary-school materials, like those from primary schools, tend to offer little more than source material for literacy workers.

They should be used with the same degree of care. Unless the learners in a literacy group specifically need to pass secondary-school exams, there is generally little value in reproducing for them the facts and information taught in schools.

Access materials

In some areas of the world, formal education has begun to explore alternative routes into the higher education system for adult students who did not have the opportunity when younger. Countries such as South Africa, which are struggling to counteract an unfair education system, are beginning to look for a shorter route to degrees and diplomas than the seven, eight, or ten years required when working through the school system. In a very few places materials have been developed especially for adult students which begin to teach the approaches and expectations of academic study.

While this material may be excellent, it is important to keep it in perspective. The formal education system, and especially higher education, takes a very specific approach to knowledge. The way in which it questions, argues, and presents information will not necessarily be appropriate for learners who are not planning to continue their studies in this way.

CHAPTER 11

'Ordinary' materials

In the previous chapter, we considered the use of 'special' materials for literacy programmes. We now turn to ways of exploiting 'ordinary' materials. The word 'ordinary' is used here to indicate the written or printed matter that already exists in the area where learners are living or working. It is the reading and the writing they will actually *need* to do and the tasks they are learning literacy *for*. While the complaint is sometimes made that this material does not exist, it is rarely the case that there is nothing at all to write or to read.

Real-life texts

Cinema notices, mail-order catalogues, advertising material, government forms, religious texts, newspapers, wrapping paper, street signs, shop names, and graffiti all fall into this category. In remote rural areas where such materials really do not exist, and there is almost nothing written in the target language of the literacy programme, literacy workers should seriously question the value of what they are asking the learners to do. Often it is a question of language choice. Is the language of the literacy class the same as that of the written notices in the area? Or are these in a different language?

Where literacy practices need to be artificially sustained, and there is no regular need to practise and use literacy skills, it is unlikely that a programme will succeed in introducing them. Research has shown that communities and individuals take on and develop those things which they feel they want or need in their lives. Literacy workers are rarely in the position of being able to create that need.

However, where ordinary materials do exist, some projects have used them creatively and adapted materials from everyday life for their own use.

Cinema posters and government forms

A literacy programme in Jaipur, India, asked learners to choose what they wanted to learn to read, and to bring their own material in with them. Instead of being given a primer, they were each offered an empty ring-binder, in which they could file the material they decided to use. If they were to operate as a group, they needed to reach agreement about

*Cinema posters in
Delhi, displaying a
wide variety of type-
faces and images.*
Photo: Rajendra Shaw

what this was, and to work on the same things at the same time.

The most popular materials that emerged from discussion were cinema notices, so the group began with these. As learning material, they had a number of advantages. Small leaflets advertising films were easily available. They used a range of type-faces, headings, and sub-headings, in different sizes; they used images as well as text, and a number of well-known names. The literacy worker was able to help the group to anticipate the words they expected to find on the poster; to recognise letters; to write the names of films; to look for specific information, such as numbers giving prices or dates; to learn to write words about the film; and to do more extensive follow-up activities. People could practise these skills by reading the larger cinema posters that decorate the billboards in the streets, and actually find out about the films they wanted to see. Gradually, as people had enough of reading cinema notices, they began to bring in other material they wanted to tackle, and moved on at their own pace.

One of the things the group wanted to do was to learn how to fill in government forms, to register births and deaths, or apply for a driving licence or a passport. The literacy worker was able to use such forms as learning materials. The group learned to write the personal details that the forms required, such as name, address, and date of birth, and discussed the presentation of the forms. Very often such forms use complicated language and are laid out in a way that is not easy for new readers to understand. Getting the group to redraft the forms in simple language before completing them provided a useful exercise in writing. It also ensured that the learners really understood the purpose of the form and what they were agreeing to. It clarified for them the relationship between a form and a contract, in which an agreement is made between two people.

The use of simpler, everyday language on official forms is a practice that is beginning to be adopted in some places. At times, literacy groups themselves have campaigned for this, by rewriting the forms and offering them as an alternative to the organisations that produced them.

Other groups have copied the format of official contracts and written a group contract for themselves. This is particularly useful in areas where literacy workers are unpaid volunteers. It makes clear for the group members what the literacy worker is prepared to offer. They in turn make clear their commitment to attend regularly, to maintain the literacy centre, and to buy their own books and pens.

Street maps and shopping lists

In Johannesburg, South Africa, a group of domestic workers wanted to learn literacy skills in English in order to improve their chances of employment. They drew up a list of tasks they would need to carry out, firstly in finding a job and then in working as domestics. These involved reading and writing addresses and then finding their way around the residential areas. One of their principal tasks would be shopping: following shopping lists, recognising shop names, reading the names on packages, and noticing the prices of different products.

This then became their learning plan and their material. They began by learning the names of streets and how to write them. They used an enlarged map of the area and tried to match addresses written on a piece of paper with the name of the street written on the map. Gradually they learned how to record information about themselves on application forms. Those in employment brought in shopping lists and packages and wrappings from products used by their employers, which in most cases were products they were not familiar with themselves. The group matched up the writing on the lists with the name on the product package, compared handwriting with type, learned to write the words they felt were useful, and read the important information from the packets. Learners invented shopping lists for each other, and went on supermarket trips to identify the packages on the shelves. Because they worked together on identifying and deciphering some of the information that surrounded them, they began to notice it everywhere they went. They were using their literacy not only in the class, but all the time.

Mail-order catalogues

In a remote village in Natal, South Africa, where literacy workers cannot obtain school books or newspapers, classes have begun to use mail-order catalogues as a source of printed texts. Factory workers who return home at weekends often bring catalogues with them to show their families what they are saving for. Mail-order companies have developed an informal network of buses or bush taxis to deliver their catalogues as widely as possible. Some learners can buy things from the catalogue, a large number cannot, but all seem to be interested in working through it.

Although catalogues contain very little extensive reading matter, using them does involve a number of complex skills. These include identifying a picture, looking up the number or letter that refers to it, and reading what are often abbreviated specifications. Actually ordering from the catalogue entails reading instructions and the 'small print' guarantees, and filling in forms. The learners were able to use them at a number of different levels. They could begin by identifying various pictures and writing the names of items. It helped the learners to understand early on that reading does not always entail reading or understanding everything on a page.

An organisation called ERA, or 'Easy Reading for Adults', produces special materials for new readers in South Africa. The staff realised that mail-order companies were far more skilled than they were in delivering their material to learners. They decided to combine with them, and asked a number of companies to include specially written stories for new readers. While this was a good use of a distribution network that already existed, in many cases what the learners actually wanted to read was the catalogues themselves. The practice of reading fiction did not previously exist in this area, and stories are regarded as something to be shared orally with a group.

Using newspapers

The University of Natal in Pietermaritzberg has begun producing a newspaper for new learners which goes out once a week with one of the larger newspapers of the area. This is distributed in the township areas, where people may buy the newspapers for the sports news. The free insert for new learners tends to get passed on and used by a member of the family who is a less confident reader. It is a form of 'distance learning': learners can practise and improve their reading and writing skills without attending a class. The insert contains activities like cross-word puzzles or gap-fill exercises, and often invites readers to write in and respond.

The insert is also used as learning material by literacy workers with groups. Some of the exercises are completed in groups, and the main articles are used to find information about the topics they discuss. However, the insert does not specifically encourage learners to move on to read the newspaper. Generally it has proved very popular; but, when asked about it, readers tended to see it as something separate from but delivered with the newspaper. It is regarded as special literacy material.

In other areas where special materials do not exist, literacy workers have used ordinary newspapers. By cutting, photocopying, reproducing, enlarging, and isolating small headlines or articles, they can focus learners' attention on a small area of text. It is good for learners' confidence to take them back to the original article within the newspaper, once they have read the enlarged version. Comparing the two helps learners to see that the literacy they are learning is part of a set of real practical skills, with which they can gain access to the written information around them.

Seed catalogues and fertiliser packages: a project that failed

In a village in Kenya, an agricultural extension project tried to introduce farmers to literacy through reading seed catalogues and the instructions on fertiliser packages. However, most of the learners were subsistence farmers, growing maize, cassava, and rice for their own consumption. Some of the migrants in the area had larger land holdings, were better educated, and were growing cash-crops. It was they who were buying agricultural chemicals, though not always fully understanding the instructions on the packages, and not using them correctly. However, as they had mostly been to school, they were not attending literacy classes.

In this case, neither the literacy programme nor the extension programme was very successful. The subsistence farmers had no interest in reading seed catalogues and little opportunity to use literacy skills. The school-based literacy which the migrant farmers had acquired as children did not really help them in using or understanding the more specialised language of written instructions. Many of them had not used their literacy skills since school, and had lost the habit. The high incidence of chemical poisoning recorded at the local hospital was largely among this group: evidently few farmers could read the warnings on the packets.

Suggestions for using 'ordinary' materials

- As far as possible, the types of materials used should be chosen by the learners themselves, and based on what is around and available.

- Learners should be encouraged to use a range of materials and to look at them in a number of different ways.

- Using different types of material helps to introduce learners to the different ways of reading and writing used in various situations.

- The same material can be used for various exercises. Most material can be used for longer than people think. If there is no new material to use, try using the same thing in a new way.

- Most material can be used intensively or extensively. Learners can focus on a letter, a word, or a line, or use the whole thing as a stimulus for further extended writing. Badly presented material can always be criticised and re-written by the group themselves.

- Try to use material which is related to the social context: things which people will find in their everyday lives. Aim to build bridges between using this material as a learning exercise and using it in a real situation.

Development materials

Agencies concerned with various aspects of development often produce their own printed materials. They generally carry messages of some sort and are based on the aim of reading to learn, rather than learning to read. They might include extension literature such as booklets on hygiene, animal husbandry, vegetable growing, bee-keeping, or family economy. They may include posters or leaflets prepared as part of a health campaign, giving information on vaccination or pregnancy or breast-feeding. In many cases these materials are produced without considering the literacy level of the population, or the ease with which they will be read. Figure 11.1 shows a pair of contrasting examples.

Figure 11.1: Health-promotion pamphlets from Nicaragua. Detailed pictures with handwritten speech bubbles, like the one above, were found to be too complicated and hard to read. Simpler images (like the one below) with typewritten words were more effective.

*Figure 11.2:
A compost pit. Is it
obvious that there is a
time lag between
adding waste
materials and water
and extracting well-
rotted compost?*

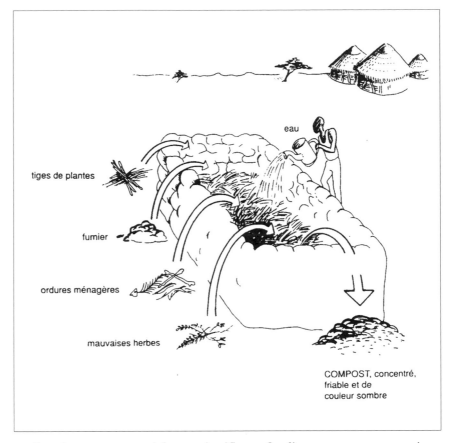

Development materials are significant for literacy programmes in a number of ways. Literacy workers may be able to offer guidelines to organisations before they produce these materials, and encourage them to field-test them with their groups and to produce them in a format which is easy to use. The conventions of technical drawing which literate people take for granted may not be immediately apparent to learners; see Figure 11.2 for an example. Groups could be encouraged to re-design the materials themselves and to evaluate the messages conveyed by them in the light of local knowledge. As printed material which is often available in remote areas, these leaflets and posters are a source of visual images, words, and information which can be read, discussed, challenged, and used in reading and writing activities.

Technical leaflets for a fisheries project

A fisheries project in Madras produced a series of technical leaflets, giving information and new ideas on ways of handling and marketing fish. The leaflets were produced to help project staff to train local people in new ways of working. They contained words and images, and were organised into stories produced as a series of points. Each point had a line illustration and a few sentences describing what was happening in the picture. The leaflets were distributed free in the area, but in many cases were under-used by the project staff. When questioned about the images, local people with limited literacy were able to understand them, but were critical of the clothes that people were wearing in the pictures. (A sari was felt to be too stylish for a working woman.) Although the leaflets were not used in literacy classes, people who saw them were already discussing the images. As the local people could identify with the characters in the pictures and were concerned with the content of the text, the leaflets could be useful in letter-identification, letter-search, word-search, and gap-fill activities, as well as serving as a stimulus to writing.

Booklets about growing vegetables

An integrated rural development project in Senegal produced a series of booklets on development-related issues which formed a staged part of a literacy campaign. When learners had completed their primers and been introduced to letters individually, they were introduced to words and then sentences about vegetable growing. The booklets were produced as stencilled copies on paper with paper covers, and lessons were carefully structured around them. A lot of thought had gone into preparing these books to follow on from the primer, but not everyone in the group was in a position to grow vegetables; others were experienced vegetable growers, but the books assumed that they knew nothing.

The stencilled text was not easy to read, and the paper covers soon became torn. Groups were moving through the book at a speed decided by the literacy worker, and repeating the words used to describe the images. They were relevant to some groups, but not to others. By providing the literacy workers with a set approach, the booklets did not encourage them to be creative in the way they worked.

Posters about breast-feeding

A health campaign in Guatemala produced posters warning of the danger of bottle-feeding babies. It contained four separate pictures, but no words. The images showed a woman looking unhappily at a bottle, a woman happily breast-feeding, a woman about to feed her child with a spoon, and the child finally spitting out the food. Although the expressions on the faces help to make the meaning of the poster clear, there is some uncertainty about what is being said. This poster was put on the wall in a literacy class and the group were invited to talk about it. They described what they thought was happening and discussed their feelings about breast-feeding. They suggested words they wanted to write and slogans for the different images. They decided on their own overall message.

Suggestions for using 'development' materials

The examples quoted above contain a number of useful lessons for using development materials.

- If the material is available, it is probably a good resource for literacy.

- No material should be used without questioning and discussing the images.

- Specially written extension material often takes no account of local knowledge, and is written in a patronising tone.

- Material written for a specific purpose and with a specific message may take no account of language level and sentence structure.

- Literacy workers and literacy learners are often in a good position to advise producers of extension material.

- The way that material is used in developing literacy skills is generally more important than what the material is.

- Information, messages, and the reproduction of images can be criticised, rewritten, or redrawn by learners. It is not necessary to accept them at their face value.

Most so-called 'post-literacy materials' are technical in nature. Much of the philosophy behind producing these materials seems to be dominated by two questions: (1) *What to do?* and (2) *How to do it?* (with a little bit of *Why to do it?* thrown in for good measure).

For example, the technician already knows that he wants people to decide to use mosquito nets soaked in an insecticide to cut down on malaria. (This is the *What to do?*) He therefore writes a pamphlet that shows *Why?* (it will cut down on malaria) and *How to?* (what to buy, what dosage to use, how long to soak the nets, etc.).

In the 'developed' world, this more resembles advertising than the thought-provoking process which properly belongs to being literate and having access to information through the written word. The problem and solution have already been identified by the experts. All that is left to do is convince the consumer to 'buy the product'.

While this type of writing has its place, and can play an important role in informing people of their options ... we should surely be more concerned with finding thought-provoking writers, ideas, and manuscripts which pose the problems without necessarily giving a single, simple solution.[21]

PART FIVE

Continuing with Literacy

Segundo Montes, El Salvador: this woman was one of a group of refugees who organised literacy classes for themselves while in exile in Honduras.
Photo: Jenny Matthews

CHAPTER 12

Developing a literate society

Literacy and change

The demand for literacy often arises as individuals and societies are beginning to change. Literacy is likely to accelerate these processes, and the experience may become uncomfortable for those in positions of power. Employees may demand better conditions. Women may demand equal treatment by men and before the law. Citizens may demand a more just political system. Inevitably, any development process carries social and political implications, as well as economic outcomes. These changes are an inevitable consequence of effective development programmes, including literacy schemes. Development workers have to be aware of them and make their own decisions about how they will react in their own particular circumstances.

In Chapter 9, we suggested that the most important test of success was whether or not the new skills had an impact outside the classroom, in the daily lives of those who were newly literate. Changes in the daily lives of the very poor, to help them achieve change for themselves, will inevitably bring about shifts in political power, as well as economic development. How development workers react to inevitable change may depend on the degree to which the original programme design was political in intent, and how the established political authorities may have viewed it.

One of the most overtly political literacy programmes was that established by Paulo Freire in Brazil in the 1960s. Many programmes today claim either to be Freirean or to use a modified Freirean approach. Freire's original work was done in the belief that literacy should enable the poor to question the situation in which they were forced to live. He believed that it was only by becoming more aware of the inequality in their lives that people would find the means to fight against it.[22]

Whether or not the various changes which accompany literacy are planned, all development workers will probably come to realise that even very local literacy programmes can and should be transforming experiences for the communities and individuals concerned. What newly literate people do with this experience is likely both to increase the *pace* of change and to change its *direction*, perhaps in ways not intended by development planners or governments. For example, a women's craft programme with a functional literacy component may not only improve product quality, but also lead to demands for a greater voice in management and marketing. How should the development agency then deal with these demands?

Continuing education

People will not develop their literacy skills unless they use them regularly. We have argued that if the only thing which learners have to read is a primer, a primer may be the only thing they end up being able to read! And if this is all that happens, then there is unlikely to be a real impact on many people's lives. On the other hand, if they practise on real materials like newspapers, government notices, advertisements, mail-order catalogues and the like, and if they go on reading them, then they have already begun to use their new skills and to develop them. The rest of this chapter looks at some of the ways in which development agencies can help to facilitate a developing literacy.

Clearly, this is easier in an environment where most people use reading and writing as part of their everyday way of doing things and of communicating with each other. In a modern city, for example, survival may depend on being able to read notices which tell you which way to go or what to do. Working or living in such an environment without being able to read or to write creates obvious problems; and people who are newly literate in those circumstances will need little extra motivation to continue developing their new skills. They are obvious candidates for any available and suitable continuing education for adults. Such provision may not be there, or may not be affordable or easily accessible. In that case, the development agency may wish to promote (or encourage governments and/or others to promote) a subject-based programme of classes in both practical subjects like tailoring and more academic subjects like language, mathematics, and economics.

However, in many parts of the developing world, especially the rural areas, writing and reading are new skills for most of the population. Visible, everyday, 'real' materials may be limited to a few advertisements or government notices or labels on items in village shops. Newspapers may be either scarce or absent. And not all, or even most, of these items will necessarily be in the language used by newly literate members of the community. In these circumstances there will be a strong argument for a programme of post-basic literacy learning — often called 'post-literacy'.

Although the term 'post-literacy' is widely used throughout the world, we, the writers of this book, try to avoid it wherever possible. There are two reasons why we take this view. The first is partly philosophical, and the second is entirely practical. We think that the use of a deceptively simple term for a rather complex set of possible programmes can be misleading. In the next few paragraphs we will try to sort out some of these complexities.

'Post-literacy' — or a developing literacy?

The first reason for questioning the apparently straightforward use of the term 'post-literacy' is the fact (which we have stressed throughout this book) that literacy itself is both complex and variable. If there is no one 'literacy', there can be no one post-literacy either. Moreover, while learning in the same class initially may perhaps be seen as appropriate for all, what learners wish to learn later will vary enormously. As we have stressed all through this book, literacy is not a simple technology which you either know how to use or do not have. Nor is it a series of stages through which people progress, from being illiterate to being literate. Whether a person is literate or not depends on context and on culture; it is a dynamic not a static state. Someone who is literate enough to read complicated language may be illiterate when it comes to using computers. Someone who can read a sophisticated novel may have problems in understanding a government form or completing an income-tax return. These examples give rise to questions like: is 'post-literacy' a course in computing or how to fill in your tax returns? The variations are endless.

At the beginning of this book, we posed four key questions.

- Who needs literacy?
- What do they need it for?
- What kind of literacy do they need?
- What is the best way to plan and implement a programme to meet those needs?

The same questions need to be asked when the basic literacy programme has been completed and people wish to move on to some kind of continuing education.

The second and entirely practical reason for viewing the term 'post-literacy' with some scepticism is that the form of organisation required to deliver a basic literacy programme is unlikely to be suitable for post-basic literacy learning. A basic programme is usually organised by trained literacy workers, and the learning takes place in regular class meetings. Once such an organisation is established, it is tempting to keep it in being for 'post-literacy' — often perceived as rather formal classes which come to look more and more like a primary school for adults.

There are two dangers here: first, that the uses of literacy in everyday life are given less prominence than the more formal literacy of the classroom; and, secondly, that a range of learning opportunities is not developed to match the learners' diverse motivations.

A support system for continuing literacy and education

A recent study of continuing literacy programmes,[23] published by the UK government's Overseas Development Administration, suggests that the best way to promote better literacy practices is to develop an effective support system, employing other helpers besides literacy practitioners. What would such a support system mean in practice, and what might it then do?

In our view, an effective support system for developing post-basic community literacy should be based on four principles of procedure.

- *It should act as a catalyst* within other programmes (such as health or income generation): it should not normally provide its own classes of instruction.

- It should attempt to *integrate improved literacy practices across all development sectors* (such as agriculture, water, health). In development jargon, it would be 'cross-sectoral'.

- It should not be aimed solely at those who have attended an initial literacy class. *It should aim to support anyone in the community who has difficulty with the reading, writing, or calculating tasks which they need to do.*

- It should *encourage the use of real literacy materials*, rather than specially prepared resources.

Real materials can be divided into two categories. The first category consists of extension materials: all those books, pamphlets, posters and the like which development agencies use to spread their message to individuals and to communities. The second consists of magazines, catalogues, advertisements, comic books and other printed materials already available but perhaps not yet widely used to improve literacy practices. Extension material is seldom used for the development of literacy, and few literacy agencies use such material for their classes, even when it is available. An effective support system would aim to exploit this rich resource.

Building a literacy support system

Support systems will vary from country to country and perhaps from programme to programme. But if it is based on the principles listed above, a support system is likely to have certain key features. First, it will be small and mobile: very different from the large, heavily staffed structures set up by some government literacy programmes. Second, it will act as a catalyst, offering advice and exercising influence among other major providers and across sectors. To do these things, it will need sufficient status, and enough funds to be able to commission small experimental projects.

All these factors point to a structure which includes:

- a small team of literacy workers, who encourage literacy practices in other sectoral programmes;
- central responsibility for the team, either in government or in a non-governmental development agency;

- some development funds for local, small-scale experimentation on a range of activities that promote literacy practices, but not for establishing separate post-basic literacy programmes.

The ODA report mentioned above[24] further suggests that the tasks of a literacy support system might include:

- training literacy practitioners to identify and use existing 'real' materials;
- bridging the gap between the producers of real materials and the users, and working with the producers of these materials to adapt them to the needs of those with literacy difficulties;
- supporting local groups in the development of new literacy agendas;
- training other professionals (such as agricultural and health workers) to help participants in their programmes with their literacy activities.

*'I'm working on a community history project. Eight of us are compiling an archive of material, and this will be our history. We work with tape recorders in pairs. A co-ordinator from the University taught us how to ask questions, and what sort of information to look for. I like this work, because it is important to remember the past and to know our history. Old people have a lot to teach us. We are also setting up a video project to record interviews with old people.' —
Esperanza Argueta, a resettled refugee in El Salvador*
Photo: Jenny Matthews

Supporting literacy in the community

A literacy support service aims to help people to use their literacy skills in their everyday lives. Finding a way to realise these aims may not be easy. Such a support system will be more difficult to organise and to implement than an initial literacy programme. There are few existing models from which to learn. The long-term needs of individuals and groups will be more varied and more complex, and even further dependent on local circumstances. Groups may have fewer long-term aims in common, as their literacy practices begin to diverge. An idea which works well in one place may not work in another. Without gathering people in a formal class, it may be more difficult to reach them and work with them in response to their emerging needs. Planners and development workers should continue to work closely with local groups and organisations, and to discuss with them the structures and facilities on which such a service might be built.

Many literacy workers agree that there is a clear need for experimental action research to find out what kind of support services would work best in different circumstances. The examples which follow are designed to give some indication of ideas and methods which planners and development workers could adapt for their own experiments.

Village library services in India and Tanzania

In Kerala (India) in the 1940s and 1950s, an independent professional association set up and developed the Kerala Library Movement, with the aim of making reading material available to people who had nothing to read. It is generally believed that this was one of the main reasons why Kerala achieved relatively high literacy rates, among men and women, compared with other Indian states. In more recent years, a state-run library service has taken over this initiative, and it has continued to grow.

In Tanzania, however, attempts to set up village libraries and to create a library service to promote reading were much less successful. There were not enough resources to produce or maintain a sufficient stock of reading material; library staff were not adequately trained; and the management of such a complex service was not established on a sound basis. In view of the difficult economic circumstances at that time, and the poor provision of basic infrastructure, it might have been more effective to run a scheme on a smaller scale.

Recycled newspapers in Uganda

In Uganda, the British agency ACTIONAID is making available old newspapers as reading material, in order to help sustain literacy. Rather than produce new books for new readers, they collect discarded newspapers in urban areas, and offer them to people who have no reading material. Newspapers use a number of different typefaces and type sizes. They contain pictures of local and national politicians whom readers may recognise. They have headlines, which can be read relatively easily, and features to be read at greater length. There are few newspapers in minority languages, but to people who are becoming literate in a national language, newspapers are a cheap and effective resource.

ALBSU and REPLAN in the UK

In the UK, there have been two examples of organisations that worked to support the development of literacy, without becoming directly involved in providing either literacy classes or on-going training. The first, operating in England and Wales, is the Adult Literacy and Basic Skills

Unit. Its function is to produce learning materials, to provide training, to encourage small projects and initiatives which investigate local needs, and to publish a regular newsletter for literacy workers and new readers. ALBSU aims to keep interest and morale high by enabling people working in small and often isolated communities to keep in touch with each other and with new ideas. It encourages organisations which provide literacy services to experiment with new ways of working. It invites bids from these organisations for financial and supervisory support, and responds to those which seem to be viable. Many of these bids are concerned with helping people to continue with their literacy, or progress on from basic literacy into other forms of continuing education. ALBSU offers advice to the providers over a limited period of time (generally two or three years), while the new initiative is being established.

The second example is REPLAN, which provided support services for those working with unemployed adults during the late 1980s.[25] REPLAN was designed to respond to changing social, economic, and political circumstances and did not prescribe any one way of working. It was concerned not only with promoting basic literacy and numeracy, but with providing education and information about education to people who needed to find paid work. The aim was to improve the life choices of individuals. Like ALBSU, REPLAN supported a number of different kinds of project that worked towards these aims. Like ALBSU, it did not offer any direct literacy provision itself, but focused on sharing ideas, resources, and materials, and publicising local projects. However, REPLAN had little or no direct funding for local initiatives. A large part of its work consisted of research into local needs and into existing provision that could be made more widely available. REPLAN workers made links between unemployed people and providers (and potential providers) of education, to try to bring the two groups together in a more efficient way. They encouraged organisations which offered education and training to consider new ways of doing it which might meet the requirements of those who needed it most. In some cases, these organisations set up pilot projects; in others they adapted existing classes. The theory was that local organisations could learn best by looking at what had been tried out in other areas, and adapting some of these ideas to fit their own circumstances. The staff encouraged organisations to contact each other, to find out what had contributed to the success or failure of an initiative.

Both ALBSU and REPLAN aimed to keep literacy workers in touch with each other, by setting up local and national networks.

Community literacy in Nepal

In Nepal, research was carried out in connection with the planning of a community literacy programme. Individuals and groups living and working in a remote hill village were questioned about the type of on-going literacy support they felt might best meet their needs.

155

Their suggestions included:

- training the owner of a local tea-shop to be able to help people to deal with the literacy tasks they had to undertake (such as reading an address or responding to a letter);

- having someone available in the local weekly market to whom people could go to check weights or calculate prices;

- offering support to individual farmers within and through a farmers' cooperative ;

- training health workers to help people to understand child-growth charts, medicine labels, prescriptions, vaccination certificates, etc. and to encourage people to use their literacy skills.

The villagers' last suggestion echoes a point made by the team of literacy experts commissioned by the Overseas Development Administration (cited above on page 151): that support for adult learners, to be most effective, 'will need to be provided more frequently *at the point of use*, rather than in special classes; and by other helpers, as well as by literacy practitioners'. Unless other development professionals come to see literacy as part of their own work too, then basic literacy on its own is unlikely to become the springboard for a truly learning and literate society.

Postscript

Be your own literacy expert

In the Preface to this book, we said that our purpose was to help development workers to listen with understanding to requests for literacy; and to provide ideas and examples for non-specialists planning a literacy programme. We will end with some words of encouragement for both these groups.

There will be high times and low times in your literacy work, and we have tried to offer some advice and some warnings. But in working through the problems that arise, the most valuable information is generally to be found on the ground. Let's look again at some of those warnings.

Literacy is more complicated than the simple mechanics of decoding letters and words

While this is true, there is no special mystery about literacy practices. How various people use literacy, what people need it for, and what sort of literacy they need will be reflected in what they currently do, and the general activities of their everyday lives. By looking at these closely, by observing how people currently carry out tasks involving calculations or keeping records or communicating over time or at a distance, the answers to these questions will become apparent. Talking to people about what they want from literacy, finding out what literacy practices exist in other places, and watching how people do things will all help in deciding what literacy is, or might be, in the particular context in which you are working.

Teaching adults is different from the way most people were taught in primary school

Sitting in rows and repeating things after a teacher may be an adequate way to memorise information, but it is seldom a good way for adults to learn to do things for themselves. If this is understood from the beginning, teaching adults is in many ways simpler than teaching children. Provided that the group and the literacy worker agree to work together as equals, sharing information, solving problems, discussing ideas, and respecting each other's knowledge and experience, then literacy workers do not need long or complex training. If you like people, relate to them well, read and write in their language, and are ready to be creative in the ways you work together, you can learn to help others learn.

There is no recipe for instant success for planners designing a literacy programme

This is true, because every context is different, and no programme will succeed if it does not take the needs of the local people into account. However, in every working situation there is information to be gathered about other development agencies working in the field, about the availability of written and printed material, about the times when people are free to attend classes and the way in which they like to learn. While this book cannot tell you how to do it, we can tell you what to look for and where to look. Once you start asking questions, further questions will invariably follow.

It's hard to work in isolation, without support from other people dealing with similar problems

But there will be people working in literacy programmes in neighbouring areas, or in extension or credit groups or non-formal education groups in the same area. Find out who those people are; get in touch with them; visit each other's groups; offer help and support to each other. Observing someone else working with a group, or watching yourself on video working with a group are two of the best ways to learn about learning. Offer to sit in with a colleague; give him or her a supportive assessment of the session; ask them to do the same for you. Point out what you feel was strong or weak about the way they dealt with the group; share information and ideas. Think about starting a newsletter or a 'round robin' letter (a handwritten letter which is circulated, to which each reader adds a few lines of information or describes a learning activity they have tried). Create your own literacy network. Learn from your own mistakes as well as other people's. Publish your failures as well as your successes!

It's hard to know what will work with a group or with a single learner: everything is a risk

But life is a risk, and at least some risks can be calculated! Ask your groups to tell you what they have learnt from the various sessions, and how things might be organised differently. Encourage an open discussion between group members. Don't assume — or allow them to assume — that you know it all. Don't be afraid of failure: only by analysing failure can we calculate success. Confidence is built up by experiencing both failure and success.

If literacy is really to be developed in a community, then all organisations will need to promote it

This may be true; but, if you start small, it may be possible to influence some of the organisations around you. Get in touch with other development agencies; share with them the information you have gathered on literacy practices and literacy needs. Find out what printed material they are producing, or what messages they are promoting. Offer to use their material or discuss their messages with your groups. Encourage your groups to be critical of anything they use; don't deliver it to them as a finished product. Share the group's comments with the other agency. Encourage the agency staff to think about how they might re-present their material or their messages in the light of these comments. Invite them in to your class. Ask for their advice; offer yours; work together.

Not everyone wants to come to literacy classes or to develop their literacy skills

For many people, the skills they already have and the strategies they currently use will be adequate for their literacy needs. But this is surely a positive and not a negative thing. Literacy alone will not change people's lives, and it is not the role of development workers to create needs in a community where there currently are none. If the environment in which people are living does not present sufficient reason for introducing literacy, then the time may not be right for a literacy programme. Those needs will arise when and if the environment changes and literacy is more widely promoted as a means of communication within the community. It is only then that the development worker will need to respond to requests for literacy.

Good luck!

Glossary of terms used in this book

Assessment
Measurement of a learner's progress. It may take the form of formal tests or less formal observations of progress, by either learner or tutor or both. 'Normed' or *norm-referenced assessment* measures progress in relation to other learners' performance. *Criterion-based assessment* measures progress according to externally based criteria (such as the concept of 'reading age', as in 'a reading age of 9'). *Ipsative assessment* measures an individual's progress from the beginning to the end of a particular educational process.

Cross-sectoral
Refers to development work which covers a number of sectors like agriculture, health, education, or community development. The encouragement of literacy is not a matter for the education sector alone.

Evaluation
The whole process of monitoring, recording, and making judgements about whether or not aims and objectives have been achieved. Evaluation which occurs during the life of a programme is said to be 'formative', because the programme can be changed as a result. Evaluation at the end of a programme is said to be 'summative', in that it summarises successes and failures in terms of the agreed aims and objectives.

Literacy and **functional literacy**
Variable concepts, not capable of precise definition. It may help to think of 'literacy' in two different ways: in terms of its role in social development (which includes purposes and context) and in terms of certain measurable skills connected with it. In practice, the two ways of looking at the concept are not separable.

UNESCO defines a literate person as one 'who can with understanding both read and write a short simple statement on his everyday life', and a functionally literate person as one able to 'engage in all those activities in which literacy is required for effective functioning of his group and community and also for enabling him to continue to use reading, writing and calculation for his own and the community's development' (UNESCO: Resolution of the General Conference, 1978).

Ideographic language
A language in which characters represent the meaning rather than the

sound of words, such as Chinese ideograms, or numbers in Roman script.

Monitoring

The systematic review and recording of what is happening during the life of a programme, as part of its evaluation.

Needs

A favourite term with professionals in the field of adult education. A concept of needs emerges out of a dialogue between development workers and communities about the wants which have been expressed.

Phonetic language

A language in which letters represent the sounds of the words and the syllables of which words are made up. Swahili and Spanish are examples of directly phonetic languages; some languages, like English, are partly phonetic.

Sustainable

One of the most recent words to enter the development vocabulary, and already in danger of over-use. A development is 'sustainable' if it persists after the external intervention is phased out. In terms of literacy, the term should probably be confined to a consideration of whether or not a particular and improved level of literacy can be sustained by factors such as greater community use of local materials (like newspapers) or the development of libraries.

Notes

1 Y. Kassam: *Illiterate No More*, Nairobi: Shungwaya Publishers, 1979.
2 Sarah Crowley: *Reading for Ourselves*, Oxford: Oxfam, 1993.
3 S.K. Battacharya: National Literacy Mission, New Delhi, 1994.
4 UNESCO/UNDP: *The Experimental World Literacy Programme, Paris: UNESCO*, 1976.
5 Paul Fordham (ed.): *One Billion Illiterates*, Toronto and Bonn: ICAE/DSE, 1985.
6 See note 5.
7 A. Gillette and J. Ryan in Paul Fordham (ed.): *Co-operating for Literacy*, Toronto and Bonn: ICAE/DSE, 1983.
8 John Fox: 'Rhetoric and Reality: A Commentary on the UNCHS Community Development Programmes in Ghana, Uganda and Zambia', Nairobi: United Nations Centre for Human Settlements (Habitat), 1993, mimeo.
9 Jules Pretty *et al.* (eds.): 'Participatory Rural Appraisal', *RRA Notes* 13, London: International Institute for Environment and Development, August 1991.
10 Paul Fordham: *Adult Education in St Vincent*, Paris: UNESCO, 1975.
11 S. Haggis: *Education for All: Purpose and Context*, Paris: UNESCO, 1992.
12 Kathleen Rockhill: 'Gender, language, and the politics of literacy', *British Journal of the Sociology of Education* 8/2, 1987.
13 'From demystification to empowerment: non-formal adult education in Pulaar in Senegal', by Sonja Fagerberg-Diallo, *Development Anthropology Network*, 11/1, Spring 1993.
14 Based on a model devised by T. Moodie in *Learning to Read, Understanding the Process*, Pinetown: Edgewood College of Education, 1986.
15 Reproduced with permission from The Teacher Development Series, ed. Adrian Underhill (Heinemann, 1994)
16 Glenys Kinnock, *The Times*, 4 February 1995.
17 Deryn Holland (1990): *The Progress Profile*, London: Adult Literacy and Basic Skills Unit (ALBSU).
18 Alan Rogers (1994), *Using Literacy: A New Approach to Post-Literacy Materials*, ODA Research Report No. 10, London: Overseas Development Administration.
19 Report of the workshop on Evaluating Empowerment in the Pilots, in 'Report of the International Workshop PRA, Literacy and

Empowerment, The Reflect Method', ACTIONAID and CAMPE, 14-17 November 1994, Bangladesh.

20 Fred Eade (1993) 'Guidelines to the Research on the Design, Layout, and Formatting of Practice Literacy Materials', ODA Report on Post-Literacy Material, London: ODA.

21 'Choosing and Publishing Books for Post-Literacy: The Experience of Pulaar in Senegal', by Sonja Fagerberg-Diallo, ARED/GIPLLN, Dakar, Senegal).

22 Paulo Freire (1976) *Cultural Action for Freedom*, London: Readers and Writers Co-operative.

23 See note 18.

24 See note 18.

25 Paul Fordham: 'Comment 1: REPLAN 1984-1991', *Studies in the Education of Adults* 24/2, October 1992.

This book has also drawn on ideas contained in the following publications:

Barton, David (1994) 'Globalisation and diversification: two opposing influences on local literacies', *Language and Education*, Vol. 8, Nos. 1 and 2

Fordham, Paul (1994) 'Language choice', *Language and Education*, Vol. 8, Nos. 1 and 2, pp. 65-8

INCED (1992) *Women's Literacy for Development*, DCE/INCED Paper 11, University of Warwick: International Centre for Education in Development

Millican, Juliet (1992) 'Women's expectations of literacy in Britain and Bangladesh', *VENA Journal* Vol. 4, No. 1

Millican, Juliet (1992) 'Integrating literacy and development: brainstorming the issues' in INCED (1992)

Rogers, Alan (1992) 'Planning and implementing literacy programmes for women' in INCED (1992)

Rogers, Alan (1994) *Women, Literacy, Income-Generation*, Reading: Education for Development

Street, Brian (1992) 'Literacy practices and the construction of gender' in INCED (1992)

INCED publications may be obtained from the Department of Continuing Education, University of Warwick, Coventry, CV4 7AL, UK.

Education for Development publications may be obtained from 'Woodmans', 7 Westwood Row, Tilehurst, Reading RG3 6LT, UK.

Further reading

Archer, David and Patrick Costello (1990) *Literacy and Power*, London: Earthscan

Asian Cultural Centre for UNESCO (ACCU) (1992) *New Guidebook for Development and Production of Literacy Materials*, Tokyo: ACCU*

Bown, Lalage (1990) *Preparing the Future. Women, Literacy and Development*, Chard: ACTIONAID*

Cammack, John (1992) *Basic Accounting for Small Groups*, Oxford: Oxfam

Crowley, Sarah (1993) *Reading for Ourselves*, Oxford: Oxfam.

Eade, Fred (1993) 'Guidelines to the Research on the Design, Layout, and Formatting of Practice Literacy Materials', ODA Report on Post-Literacy Material, London: ODA

Fuglesang, Andreas (1982) *About Understanding: Ideas and Observations on Cross-cultural Understanding*, New York: Dag Hammerskjold Foundation

Gajanayake, Stanley and Jaya Gajanayake (1993) *Community Empowerment. A Participatory Training Manual on Community Project Development*, Dekalb: Northern Illinois University*

Holland, Deryn (1990) *The Progress Profile*, London: Adult Literacy and Basic Skills Unit (ALBSU)

Holland, Deryn (1988) *Developing Literacy and Numeracy: An Intermediate Pack for Trainers*, Milton Keynes: The Open University

Hutton, Barbara (1992) (ed) *Adult Basic Education in South Africa*, Cape Town: Oxford University Press

Jennings, James (1990) *Adult Literacy: Master or Servant?*, Dhaka: University Press.

Lind, Agneta and Anton Johnston (1990), *Adult Literacy in the Third World*, Stockholm: SIDA

Lyster, Elda (1992) 'Current approaches to first language methodology' in Hutton (ed) (1992)

Millican, Juliet (1991) *Reading, Writing and Cultivating: A Handbook for Post-Literacy Workers, Based on Experiences in Senegal*, The Hague: CESO

Rogers, Alan (1992) *Adults Learning for Development*, London: Cassell

Rogers, Alan (1994) *Women, Literacy, Income-Generation*, Reading: Education for Development

Rogers, Alan (1994) *Using Literacy: A New Approach to Post-Literacy Materials*, ODA Research Report No. 10, London: Overseas Development Administration

Street, Brian (1993) *Cross-Cultural Approaches to Literacy*, Cambridge: Cambridge University Press

• These publications may be obtained free of charge by applicants from developing countries. Write to the Institute for International Co-operation of the German Adult Education Association, IIZ/DVV, Obere Wilhelmstrasse 32, D-53225, Bonn. IIZ/DVV also publishes the half-yearly journal *Adult Education and Development*, which gives wide coverage to adult literacy.

Index

VSO Books

VSO Books is the publishing unit of Voluntary Service Overseas. More than 20,000 skilled volunteers have worked alongside national colleagues in over 55 countries throughout the developing world in the last 35 years. VSO Books draws upon this range of experience to produce publications which aim to be of direct, practical use in development. Care is taken to present each area of volunteer experience in the context of current thinking about development.

A wide readership will find VSO books useful, ranging from development workers, project implementers, and teachers to project planners, policy-makers, and ministry officials in both the South and the North.

Current publications include:

The Science Teachers' Handbook

Andy Byers, Ann Childs, and Chris Laine, 128 pp, paperback, VSO/Heinemann; ISBN 0 435 92301 1
The Science Teachers' Handbook contains exciting and practical ideas for demonstrating science in even the least-resourced classroom. VSO teachers and their colleagues around the world have developed these ideas to bring Biology, Chemistry, and Physics to life, using creativity and simple, locally available materials. This book is a valuable reference for new and experienced science teachers at Junior and Secondary levels.

Setting Up and Running a School Library

Nicola Baird, 137 pp, paperback, VSO/Heinemann; ISBN 0 435 92304 8
This book is ideal for librarians and teachers setting up and running a library on limited resources. It is a lively and practical guide, covering all aspects of running a school library. Drawing upon the experience of teachers all over the world, it provides step-by-step information, particularly useful for teachers (and others) not trained as librarians. Even with few resources, this book shows that it is possible to set up a library which will make a real difference.

and forthcoming ...

How to Make and Use Visual Aids

Nicola Baird and Nicola Harford, approx. 132 pp, paperback, VSO
This highly illustrated, practical manual covers a comprehensive list of common types of visual aid and offers variations and tips on how to make and use them in low-resource situations. This book is suitable for teachers and trainers across a wide range of development fields, in both formal and informal educational settings.

For more information about current and forthcoming titles, please contact:

VSO Books,

Voluntary Service Overseas,

317 Putney Bridge Road,

London

SW15 2PN,

UK

tel. (+44) 0181 780 2266;

fax (+44) 0181 780 1326

Oxfam Publications

Oxfam (UK and Ireland) works with poor people, regardless of race or religion, in their struggle against hunger, disease, exploitation, and poverty in over 70 countries around the world, through relief, development, and research overseas and public education at home. Oxfam publishes a wide range of books, manuals, and resource materials for specialist, academic, and general readers.

Current publications include:

Reading for Ourselves

Sarah Crowley, 24 pp, paperback, ISBN 0 85598 201 2
Millions of adults around the world cannot read or write. *Reading for Ourselves* is about some of these people, and their struggle for literacy and numeracy. In their own words, learners from six countries describe the difference which proficiency has made to their lives. This illustrated collection of case-studies is mainly intended as an accessible reader for adult literacy students, but it also offers an introduction to the role of literacy in development.

Basic Accounting for Small Groups

John Cammack, 64 pp, paperback, ISBN 0 85598 148 2
A step-by-step guide to basic accounting and financial management techniques for those with no previous experience of accounting and book-keeping, this book is ideal for any small group which needs to keep accurate records of its financial transactions.

and forthcoming ...

Education and Training for Refugees and Displaced People

Oxfam Development Guideline No. 10
Barry Sesnan, approx. 192 pp, paperback, ISBN 0 85598 313 2; hardback, ISBN 0 85598 312 4
In any emergency which involves the long-term displacement of large groups of people, there is a demand for education. Often refugees themselves set up a rudimentary system of primary education and ask for support; or there is pressure from individuals for higher education and scholarships. The support agency usually wants to help, but field-workers often lack the relevant expertise. Drawing on a wide range of case-studies, this book gives practical advice for dealing with such situations. It also considers issues of policy, such as access and quality. It suggests that displacement may be an opportunity as well as a crisis: notably in enabling women and girls to gain access to education.

For more information about current and forthcoming titles, please contact:

Oxfam Publishing,

274 Banbury Road,

Oxford OX2 7DZ,

UK

tel. (+44) 01865 313172;

fax (+44) 01865 313235

170